£3.

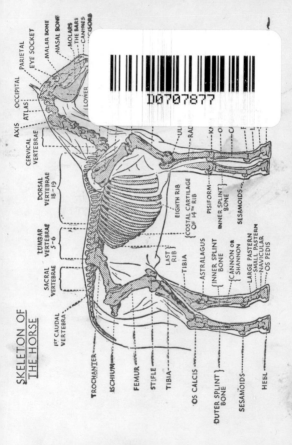

SKELETON OF THE HORSE

OCCIPITAL PARIETAL EYE SOCKET MALAR BONE NASAL BONE
THE BARS CANINES INCISORS MOLARS
(LOWER

AXIS ATLAS CERVICAL VERTEBRAE

DORSAL VERTEBRAE 18-19

ULNA RADIUS

EIGHTH RIB
(COSTAL CARTILAGE OF 14TH RIB

LUMBAR VERTEBRAE 5-6

SACRAL VERTEBRAE

LAST RIB

PISIFORM
INNER SPLINT BONE
SESAMOIDS

1ST CAUDAL VERTEBRA

ASTRALAGUS
{INNER SPLINT BONE
CANNON OR SHANNON

KNEE
CARPAL

TIBIA

LARGE PASTERN
SMALL PASTERN
NAVICULAR
OS PEDIS

TROCHANTER

ISCHIUM

FEMUR

STIFLE

TIBIA

OS CALCIS

OUTER SPLINT BONE

SESAMOIDS

HEEL

THE OBSERVER'S BOOK OF

HORSES
AND PONIES

By
R. S. SUMMERHAYS

Describing
ONE HUNDRED AND EIGHT
BREEDS AND VARIETIES
with 81 illustrations

FREDERICK WARNE & CO. LTD.
LONDON AND NEW YORK

FREDERICK WARNE & CO. LTD.
LONDON
ENGLAND
1948

© REVISED EDITION
FREDERICK WARNE & CO. LTD.
1958

Reprinted 1959
Reprinted 1960

R. S. SUMMERHAYS, Compiler of "Summerhays' Encyclopaedia for Horsemen," Author of " From Saddle & Fireside," "Here's Horse Sense," "Elements of Riding," "Elements of Hunting," "Riding for All," "The Problem Horse," etc., Past President of The Arab Horse Society, The National Pony Society and International Horse Judge.

Printed in Great Britain

PREFACE

FROM time to time volumes of considerable size and much detail have been produced on the subject of the Horses and Ponies of the world. It is believed that never before has the subject been compressed within the compass of a book which can be carried in a man's pocket.

The scope of the book being such, the description of each breed needs to be much concentrated. The aim has been to deal in the briefest form with the origin and development of each breed, while at the same time giving a word-picture of its appearance and general character ; and, where it exists, the official description issued by the appropriate Breed Society.

Over 100 breeds and varieties have been dealt with—a particularly impressive number when it is considered how few of these may be looked upon as pure or truly indigenous breeds. Many more breeds or types might have been included ; but in each case, after careful consideration and research, it was found that the breed under review was too similar to some other dealt with in these pages, and probably came from the same country.

There is no doubt that the greater number of horses and ponies in the world, though bearing a breed name and, indeed, considered as a distinct breed, are, in fact, part-bred. These, in the main, have been graded-up or refined from probably native stock for some specific purpose, such as to meet the agricultural or urban requirements of the country. Before many pages have been turned the reader will be impressed by the world-wide influence in this grading-up of the Arab and the English Thoroughbred, and it can

3

be generally asserted that where this process has been seriously practised, then inevitably recourse has been had to one or other, and frequently both, of these famous breeds.

A noticeable fact is the strong liking which Americans have for the colourful in horse-breeding, for in America are found, registered and generally fostered by their respective Breed Societies, the Pinto, the Palomino, the Appaloosa and the Criollo. Their example might well be followed, for apart from their picturesque appearance these breeds have much worth in themselves.

The horse population has decreased steadily for many years, but the basic requirements of man for the horse will one day become stabilised, for as the horse has always served man for his pleasure and daily needs, so will he continue to do.

My very grateful thanks are offered to Lt.-Col. C. E. G. Hope and Lt. K. Rutczynski for their great help to me in compiling this work, also to Mrs. Juanita Berlin and Dr. C. W. Grote for their assistance.

Acknowledgements are also due to Mr. Wayne Dinsmore of the, now non-existent, Horse and Mule Assn. of America for certain photographs ; to the Hayes Estate and Messrs. Hurst and Blackett for photographs reproduced from *Points of the Horse* ; to the *New South Wales Gazetteer* and *Indian Farming*, to Lady Wentworth, Capt. M. H. Hayes, Col. D. O. Phillott, Maj.-Gen. Sir James Johnstone, Prof. Janikowski, E. Iverton and A. E. Pease, from whose works I have quoted.

R. S. SUMMERHAYS.

THE HORSE-BREEDING COUNTRIES OF THE WORLD

THE AMERICAS AND CANADA. In spite of its vast area, Canada never has been and, presumably, never will be a country for extensive breeding of horses. As is the case with most countries, except those subjected to great extremes of temperature or where the general run of the soil is against the production of forage suitable for feeding animals, the breeding of horses does in fact take place, but this is in parts where the temperature is more equable. Nothing is carried on, however, on a very large scale, and certainly such breeding as there is does not approach to anything in the nature of a national industry.

That horses, in the main, thrive in Canada and are not subject to disease such as they are in some parts of the world is certain. The fact that the winters are very severe is, from a health point of view, rather advantageous than otherwise to the horse. None the less, this great cold and the comparative shortness of the spring and summer months are factors that are against the encouragement of horse-breeding. It is for this reason, perhaps as much as any, that Canada cannot claim as her own any particular race of horse. Therefore we have to cross the border and go farther south before we come to the land where the horse is bred in great numbers, and where, too, definite breeds and types are considerable in number. In the pages of this book will be described the many different breeds to be found not only in the United States but also farther south still—in South America.

We will, therefore, proceed south and deal first with the United States of America as a horse-breeding country. It seems fairly certain (and popular belief would be disappointed if it was proved to the contrary) that Christopher Columbus was responsible for the introduction of the horse into America. This is probably so ; but it is, however, certain that the early settlers in the North American continent found it imperative to introduce, and did in fact import, horses into America. In this book will be found much information in regard to the type of horses and their origin, but in this particular section we are in the main concerned with the advantages, or otherwise, which the United States offers to the breeder of horses. We know that North America is great in area and, in consequence, varied in climate. We know, too, that on its western side great mountain ranges abound, but this is not the country for breeding horses. There are, however, in other parts fertile plains most generously watered and possessed of herbage very admirably suited to the growth of cattle and horses. It was over such plains as these that, centuries ago, herds of horses ran wild, at times increasing to such an extent that they became a menace. What interests us is that climate, soil and the care-free life were ideal for growing the hardy horse—which they certainly did. Civilisation, however, pursued its relentless course, and the great herds of horses are no longer, whilst the grazing areas, though still existing, are much reduced in size.

It may be assumed, therefore, that this great continent enjoys certain extensive areas which are ideal for the growth of the horse at its best, and very proudly does it claim the picturesquely named " Blue Grass Country " of Kentucky, which may roughly be described as lying mid-east. Here is to be found the ideal nursery for the horse, and here, too, there are found the great horse-breeding establishments, for it is the home of the flat-racer and trotting horse, as well as many other of America's breeds. Much could be written of this fertile land, but the great advantage it offers to the horse breeder is that its rainfall is adequate without being excessive, and seems to precipitate fairly evenly throughout the year. Manures and artificial fertilisers are all very well, but in Kentucky, with Lexington as a centre, there is a soil containing that amount of lime which permits the growth of grass at its best and, what is so important, the phosphate to stimulate such growth. It is claimed, indeed, that the best land round about Lexington has from six to ten times as much available phosphate as some of the best corn-growing soils in the States. Indeed, the soil is so rich in phosphate that no advantage accrues whatever by the addition of phosphate fertilisers.

We have dealt with the country as a whole and the Blue Grass Country of Kentucky in particular, but the United States can fairly claim that the horse can be bred with satisfaction in the greater part of that country.

When we think of the southern half of the Americas, that great continent of South America, our thoughts instinctively turn to the Criollo, the polo pony and the cow pony, three indispensable, immensely tough and indefatigable workers on the estancias. A great part of South America can rightly claim to be a horse-growing country, and, except in the great mountains on the western side and where the extremes of temperature are too pronounced, the horse does grow with great advantage to the breeder. History seems to emphasise this fact, for we are told that the Spanish Expedition of Pizarro, engaged in the conquest of Peru, had 21 horses, which certainly must have bred at an astonishing rate, for it is known that some twenty years later vast herds of these were found in the country bounding the south shore of the Rio de la Plata. Perhaps it was that these horses found other wild herds and intermingled with them, but this only goes to confirm the fact that the horse thrives in its wild state in that country.

So long as cattle continue to be grown in the semi-wild state, roaming at large over big tracts of country, as distinct from the farm-bred animal, so will the horse be used in large numbers in South America. There has always been a considerable trade in the Argentine polo pony, but what future lies in store for this animal cannot be foretold. It owes so much of its intelligence and handiness to the fact that it has either been used as a cow pony or the skill and wiles of that pony are bred in it. Whatever demands may be made upon the country in the years to come, the fact remains that South America always has been and will remain, though perhaps in diminishing importance, a great country for the breeding and rearing of horses.

ASIA. In the description of the breeding grounds of the horse under this title we include primarily the following countries : Arabia, Syria, Persia, Turkestan, Mongolia and Northern India. It is generally considered that this was the original breeding area of the horse as we know him now. He is also found in other parts of Asia—China, Burma, Assam, Malaya, Java, Sumatra—but it is fairly certain that he came there as an immigrant and was not indigenous to those countries. John Crawford records in his " History of the Indian Archipelago " (1820) that the horse was still unknown in many of the islands. As far back as 1345 that great traveller Ibn Batuta found no horses in Java. It is generally accepted that the ponies of Java and Sumatra, the Batak or Deli— names derived from the Batak range of hills in Sumatra where they are bred and the port of Deli from which they are exported to Singapore— are of Arabian and Persian origin. In the 13th and 14th centuries there was considerable traffic between Arabia and Persia and India and South-east Asia. Similarly the China pony is really a cross between the Mongolian and foreign stock. The ponies of Burma, the Shan States, and Manipur, although very ancient breeds, appear to take their origin from the horse of Mongolia.

Remains of a horse with a skull very similar in some characteristics to that of the Arab have been found in Pliocene deposits of the Siwaliks, the southern foothills in India of the Himalaya. The other prehistoric horse of India is one whose remains were found in the more recent Pleistocene deposits of the valley of the Narbada in Central India, but it is impossible to say for certain whether or not this is an ancestral type of the onager or wild ass, rather than of the horse.

Meanwhile, we are certain of two types, the Mongolian horse and the Arab. From all the evidence these appear to be the two main sources of the two main original blood-streams of the horse in the Old World. Certainly these are the two strains which have impressed their types most firmly on the majority of our modern horses.

The Mongolian influence has spread all over Central Asia, China, Turkestan, the Himalayas, India and the tropical and sub-tropical countries of Asia and Burma, and to Russia and Northern Europe. The Arab blood has flowed to India and South-east Asia, and westwards via North Africa into Europe. The strains probably met in India and in Persia, the horses of which seem to have descended from those of Turkestan (ex-Mongolian) on the one side and from those of Arabia on the other.

Considering now the geographical and climatic effect of this vast area on the horse, it roughly divides itself into three types of country : the deserts and plains of the west and south-west— Arabia, Persia, Northern India, with great extremes of heat and cold, but generally speaking with hot, dry climates ; the highlands and plateaux of Central Asia, wind-swept and bitterly cold ; and the tropical and sub-tropical regions of South-east Asia—Burma, Malaya, Java, Sumatra, with their extreme humidity and little variation of temperature.

The first two areas had—and still have—one common feature which made them suitable for the horse, wide, open spaces where the horse could roam at large and use his speed to escape from his enemies.

The country is generally arid, with wide areas of desert and barren country, stony of soil and containing a certain amount of limestone, on which, as we know, the Horse has always flourished most happily. Grazing and fodder is generally scarce except in oases and cultivated districts ; but in all these countries, Arabia especially, a good crop of grass and herbage always springs up after rain. The ground is stony, sandy, or iron hard.

The western area, with its hot, sunny climate—temperatures reach over 120° in the shade in summer—has produced *par excellence* what is known as the hot-blooded horse, with fine lines, flat or concave faces—the latter notably of course in the Arab—and with eager, fiery, generous temperaments, light of build and fleet of foot. The northern area has produced a less spectacular creature, heavier in build, and slower of movement. In these regions the temperature varies from an average of 15° F. in January to 64° F. in July. The plains are swept by fierce winds and there is little rainfall. In the north abound great forests of larch, cedar, pine and so on ; in the south, in river valleys, there are rich pasture and prairie lands ; farther south still the high plateaux are desolate and treeless, with very scanty pasture. The horses of the third area take their characteristics from their ancestors from the first two. The features of this area are, as we have seen, extreme humidity with temperatures averaging from 90° to 100°, dense jungle and close, thick, bushy country, which is most unsuitable for horses ; consequently they only really flourish in the highlands of these regions.

All these different types of country and climate have had the same effect on the horses bred in them, namely, to keep them small and to make them at the same time extremely hardy. Captain M. H. Hayes (" Points of the Horse," Ch. XVII) wrote :

Horses attain their greatest height in temperate climates and diminish in size in cold climates and also in hot ones. In defining the limits of temperature for climates which are suitable for horses, we may roughly state that they should be not colder than the low-lying lands of Scotland or hotter than the south of France. Differences in temperature are produced as a rule by latitude or altitude or by a combination of these two causes. . . . As an instance of reduction in height produced solely by high altitude, we have the twelve-hand Batak pony, which is bred in Sumatra, on or close to the Equator, but on high mountains. The fact that he is largely crossed with Arab blood does not free him from the effect of his cold climate. This dwarfing influence of a high altitude is well shown by the small size of Himalayan ponies, such as those of Bhutan, Nepal and Spiti. Cold, in diminishing heights produces this effect, chiefly in reducing the length of the limbs, but it does not decrease the animal's vigour to any appreciable extent. Thus the Finnish, Mountain Welsh, Shetland, Batak and Himalayan ponies are shortlegged, hardy and strong for their size. Excess of climatic heat, on the contrary, reduces the size of the body to a much greater extent than the length of the limbs, and consequently diminishes the animal's comparative strength.

On humidity also, he says :

Evaporation of perspiration plays a very large part in keeping the horse's body cool during hot weather, and its rapidity varies in inverse proportion to the amount of moisture which is in the atmosphere. Hence its cooling and health-preserving influence is more or less nullified in climates which are hot and moist. Thus we find that in the moist and warm climate of Egypt, horse-breeding is such a failure that horses have to be largely imported, chiefly from Syria.

These are not the only influences which affect the horse, and another most important factor is feeding and pasturage. Again, Captain Hayes writes :

The amount of moisture in pasture upon which horses are brought up for many generations greatly affects their conformation. Thus we find that heavy cart-horses are produced, under natural conditions, only in districts where the herbage is succulent. . . . Saddle and light harness horses, on the contrary, thrive best on comparatively dry soil. . . . During all my travels I have never seen a natural breed of heavy draught horses produced on dry soil.

And it may be remarked here that all attempts to establish a firm breed of Indian country-bred without the continual introduction into every other generation of British blood has failed. After the second generation the progeny begin to revert in size and appearance to the original type. Nor, so far as we know, has the horse ever been seriously used for draught in India, his place invariably being taken by oxen.

It is interesting to note what substitutes for forage are used by the inhabitants of India, Persia and Arabia. Along the Persian Gulf fish and dates are a regular horse diet, and they seem to thrive on it. In parenthesis, a common diet in

Baluchistan for a sick camel is a whole boiled chicken ! As Colonel D. C. Phillott says :

Indian country-breds (and horses in other parts of Asia too, for that matter) will eat and thrive on food that would probably kill English horses and cattle ; in Tibet the Tanghans are given pig's blood and raw liver ; and in the cold regions of Central Asia meat is regarded as a necessity for horses.

To sum up, Western and Central Asia were by climate and geography well suited, up to a point, to be a breeding-ground for the horse. The limitations imposed by temperature and pasturage, in spite of the essential limestone in the soil, produced the horse best adapted to survive in these regions—small, fast, tough and wiry, with feet like iron and a body that does not need a vast amount of food to keep it going.

A very similar type of terrain, the North African, should be included in this survey, from which has come the Libyan horse, the Barb, and which was certainly one of the routes by which the Arab reached Europe. The south-western and tropical regions did not produce an indigenous horse, and the one that was introduced remained small in size and generally of thicker and of more solid build than that of the open desert spaces.

It is impossible to go into much detail in a short survey such as this, but enough has been said, perhaps, to give a general idea of the vast area and of the horses it has produced, and where the horse was first tamed. It may be interesting to note that the earliest known written literature of the horse is believed to come from Mesopotamia, the Hittite " Handbook for the Treatment

of the Horse," which appeared inscribed on six
clay tablets about 1360 B.C. The book deals with
the care of the horse used for war and racing
chariots. When one considers the labour involved
in the production of such a work, the interest
taken in the horse even then must have been
great indeed.

AUSTRALASIA. The horse is bred now in all
parts of Australasia, but attention will necessarily
be concentrated on Australia as the principal
breeding-ground of the horse in the Antipodes.
It is interesting to note that all this area, which is
so admirably adapted for the breeding and main-
tenance of the horse, had never known one until
it was introduced by man at the end of the 18th
century.
The general physical formation of Australia is
a coastal plain rising fairly easily to barrier ranges
of mountains, a good deal higher in the east than
in the west, with an enormous central plain, partly
waterless desert and partly scrub, and a moderately
high cultivable and habitable plateau in the hinterland of the State of Western Australia. The
coastal plains and highlands of the east, on either
side of the mountain barriers, are generally well-
watered and temperate in climate, have wide
ranges with good and varied pasture, and plenty
of limestone in the soil. It is here that the
" Waler," the horse of Australia, has reached its
highest pitch of breeding and performance,
especially in the State of New South Wales, and
to a lesser extent in Queensland and Victoria.
In the " New South Wales Agricultural
Gazetteer " we read :

The climate, natural features, soil and pasture in the country known as the Western Slopes of New South Wales—that is, the hilly and undulating country, not the mountainous—on the west side of the Great Dividing Coast Range, which extends from the southern to the northern boundary of the State, is such as to render it superior to almost any other part of the world for horse breeding, except, perhaps, some tracts of similar country in the neighbouring States of Victoria and Queensland.

The climate is essentially temperate, neither too hot nor too cold, and the winter being mild and short, the condition of the stock in the pasture, when it is sufficient, is scarcely reduced at all by the cold. The hilly and undulating formation of the country, again, with here and there strips of hard and stony ground and with plenty of fallen timber, develop the muscles of the horse and also give him good wind, sound hoofs, and free and safe action, while the timber and brush in the hollows and gullies afford the necessary shelter from the cold westerly and south-westerly winds. With this shelter, and plenty of nutritious grass in the lower ground, and the nice sweet pickings of which the horses are so fond in the light fertile rises, and sufficient water, this portion of New South Wales supplies all that a horse can desire in ordinary favourable seasons. There are not a few localities where horses have the benefit of a limestone formation.

It is here, on this eastern side of Australia, that practically every variety of English light and heavy horse of good size is produced, and here, of course, that racing flourishes. Australia, moreover, is the home *par excellence* of the high jumper. Horses from Australia always thrived in India, and were exported in large numbers as cavalry and artillery remounts and racehorses.

In Western Australia the climate is very dry,

subject to great extremes of temperature, and tends to resemble to some extent that of Arabia and North India. The mean temperature on the coast in January–February—the antipodean summer—is 80°–85° F. Farther inland, however, and in certain parts of Central Australia the day temperatures tend to be very high, reaching 110°–113° F., with a considerable drop after sundown. There is plenty of good grazing and scrub land and good limestone content in the soil. The horses of Western Australia are descendants of the Java and East Indian pony, having been imported from Timor and elsewhere, and remain small in size and peculiar to this part of Australia.

We can see in this difference of size between the horses of eastern and western Australia the operation of the effect of temperature on size, the animals of the more temperate east growing to full size and those of the west remaining as ponies. As Captain M. H. Hayes has said : " Horses attain their greatest height in temperate climates, and diminish in size in cold climates and also in hot ones." (This subject is considered more fully in the article on Asia as a breeding ground.)

New Zealand also has favourable climatic and geographical conditions for the breeding of horses : wide ranges, good rolling grass lands with excellent pasturage and limestone content ; but horse-breeding has never been the serious business there that it became in Australia. Actually horses were introduced into New Zealand at about the same time as they were to Australia, and a fair amount of stock came from

Australia itself. With such favourable conditions New Zealand has thus been able to produce good types of pony and light horse and a fine breed of pure Clydesdale.

THE BRITISH ISLES AND EIRE. On the whole better-favoured than any other part of the world, the British Isles has always been a great country for the breeding of horses. No doubt such a happy position is largely due to the climate which it enjoys—or perhaps suffers—where normally no extremes of heat are met with and where there is abundant moisture to encourage the growth of rich grasslands, for the soil, even without much artificial attention, tends to grow grass both nutritious and abundant. Pastures unless emanating from a limestone base are deficient in those qualities which tend to produce in horses (and do in fact undoubtedly produce) that bulk and density of bone which is of such primary importance to their work and well-being. For, indeed, without such any horse or pony, however good may be its conformation, tends to melt away under the stress and strain of hard work.

The British Isles are unique in all the countries of the world in having so many truly indigenous breeds. Moreover, it is a remarkable fact that in these small islands there are no fewer than nine breeds each one not only indigenous to a particular district, but in appearance each is dissimilar. They have, however, characteristics which they share in common, those of small size, of great hardiness, surefootedness, intelligence and the ability to feed and thrive where most other horses would starve. These breeds are the

Shetland and Highland of Scotland, the Fell and Dales of northern England, the Welsh Mountain Pony from Wales, the Exmoors and the Dartmoors from the extreme south-west, and the New Forest from southern England. Ireland can claim only one indigenous breed, the good Connemara.

Scotland has never laid claim to being a country where the breeding of horses is a profitable venture, for the climate is, generally speaking, too severe. In the main it is only the breeds such as the Shetland and Highland which manage to stand up to the climate, and they certainly do so in brave fashion. We must not, however, forget the Clydesdale, that massive but active agricultural and commercial horse, which emanated from the south of Scotland. The Clydesdale is still bred in large numbers, and is the pride of Scotland, and it would seem that its home pastures give it all that which helps to grow a good horse.

Travelling south, we come to those famous horse-breeding grounds the Ridings of Yorkshire. Thoroughbreds, Hunters, the Yorkshire Coach Horse and the Cleveland Bay, not to mention the famous Hackney, have come in great numbers from those well-named broad acres of Yorkshire. If we travel still farther south, there can be little said against most of the " shires " as nurseries for any horses you may like to breed there. This would include, therefore, the heavy breeds, for those parts are the home of England's mammoth Shire horses.

The Eastern Counties have always favoured the breeding of the clean-legged cart-horses, for there is the home of the Suffolk, or Punch, as he is affectionately called, while the Percheron, a comparatively new importation, has set his impressive and worthy bulk firmly into the roots of East Anglia. Most important of all, the Eastern Counties have within their borders Newmarket, the headquarters of racing and the very home of the world-famous English Thoroughbred. From its classic paddocks Newmarket has sent the finest racehorses the world has ever seen, and the name "Newmarket" is synonymous with racing and the racehorse at its best.

Little detailed reference need be given to the southern part of England. The climate there is generally looked upon as being the more genial, and throughout its length and breadth, except perhaps in the extreme south-west, are to be found many famous thoroughbred studs and training establishments, including in particular those to be found tucked away in the rolling Wiltshire Downs and the glorious South Downs which strike across the southern part of Sussex.

England with her equable climate favours and fosters the horse, for there through the energy and enthusiasm of her people and their proverbially great love of the horse the breed is nurtured with care and great understanding and is found at its best.

In this general survey of the horse-breeding countries, it can be said with confidence that no country in the world has a greater reputation for breeding the best horses than has Ireland, and by this I mean the best-boned and the most healthy and the most desirable horses to breed from, for there is in the soil and climate of Ireland all that which seems to produce the best. Small wonder, therefore, that buyers from all over the world, particularly from the Continent, have in the past always gone to Ireland, being assured that there their demands would be supplied. Spread over the years the export of horses from that country has been enormous.

The most favoured part of Eire is the south-east, where great numbers of thoroughbreds have been foaled and where the best of that typical Irish horse, the part-bred hunter type, has been bred. Perhaps most famous of all Ireland's contribution to the horse world has been, and still is, the steeplechaser.

Less favoured is the north and the west of Ireland, although great numbers of horses are bred there, and the latter is, of course, the home of the Connemara Pony.

EUROPE. Although it is difficult to make any definite statements as to the origin of the horse, it seems that all in their wild state belonged in the main to four types which each in time developed into the different breeds as we know them today.

Two of these types, the " hot-blood " horse, or oriental, and the Mongolian steppe horse, come from Asia ; while the heavy " cold-blood " horse and the North European (also called the " forest " horse) have Europe as their cradle. Later, the influence of man, who was responsible for taking the horses from their original regions and attempting to adapt them to their new conditions, also that of soil and climate, which are decisive elements, caused many changes in their size, shape, skeleton, conformation and general character. Thus new breeds were created which were kept pure or crossed. Nevertheless, we can always classify them as belonging to one of the four above-mentioned principal types of horses, with the addition of the type of a so-called " warm-blood " horse which was formed through crossing " cold-bloods " with " hot-bloods."

Typical representatives of the " hot-bloods " are : Barb, Arab, and the latter's derivative, the English Thoroughbred. It is not necessary to deal with a detailed description of this type, which will be found later under the description of each breed. What should be emphasised, however, is that this type of horse, which originally came from the Middle East, today is bred with the greatest care all over Europe—and indeed the world—not only for providing to the comparatively small group of racegoers the thrill of sport and betting, but as priceless and most necessary material for the improvement of European local breeds employed for military and agricultural purposes. Especially do they play a very important role in the countries where a great number of cavalry horses are required or the local conditions, such as long distances, bad roads or lack of machinery in agriculture, make the light horse necessary as a working horse.

In Germany, where a strong, active horse was required for both military service and general use, a " hot-blood " horse of the species of the English Thoroughbred and, to a lesser degree, the Arab, was crossed with " cold-blood " breeds, thus resulting in " warm-blood " German breeds such as Hanover, Trakehnen, Holstein, Beberbeck and Oldenburg.

In Hungary new half-breeds, such as Nonius

and Gidrans, were created with the help of the English Thoroughbred, while Shagya was based on Arabian blood.

In France the English Thoroughbred is responsible for the formation of Anglo-Norman and varieties of so-called *Demi sang du Centre* (Limousin and Charolais), while Arabian influence predominates *Demi sang du Midi* (Tarbenian Horse).

In Poland the majority of horse stock are half-bred horses with a strong saturation of oriental blood, while in many provinces the standard of English half-bred as the horse of general use is established. That is why Poland, which occupies in Europe the leading place with Russia (which can hardly be called a European country) as far as the number of horses is concerned, breeds the greatest number of " hot-blood " horses.

In Russia the English Thoroughbred was once used to a large extent to increase the size and to improve generally the Mongolian steppe horses, which are too small as cavalry remounts or agricultural horses (Anglo-Kozakh).

It is also worth mentioning that " hot-blood " horses such as Arab, Barb, Persians and Turkish, which were brought by invaders to Europe centuries ago, were responsible for the creation of some of the older European breeds, such as the Polish (which unfortunately died out), Spanish Jennet and, through the latter, the Kladruber and Neapolitan horse.

The " cold-blood " horse has as its cradle the fertile plains of North-west Europe, which extend either on the sea-shores or in the valleys of big rivers. This horse, living on the succulent herbage abundant in nutritive salts and in mild climate conditions, grew to a large, powerful and massive animal, free from the attacks of wild animals such as preyed upon the desert or steppe horse. Neither was it subjected to trials of speed and endurance, thus tending to become rather heavy and phlegmatic. Today they are seen not only in their original regions, natural conditions of which favour their growth and the building-up of their powerful muscular frames, but they went to big industrial centres or agricultural districts, where their great power of traction, increased by their weight, made them economic and valuable workers. Thus the Percheron lives and is bred not only in Perche or in Belgium—which breeds perhaps the best Percheron—but in many other parts of Europe and the world. In the same way the Ardennes is the most popular breed in Sweden, where, together with the North-Swedish horse, they are found to be very useful in the forestry industry. Even countries whose natural conditions do not favour the breeding of the " cold-blood " horse, nevertheless established on special farms breeding-centres for Ardennes, Brabançons and Vladimir Clydesdales, which, moreover, are used for crossing with lighter breeds where a heavier horse is needed.

The biggest European centres for breeding the " cold-blood " horse in all his many varieties remain the same, and are placed for the most part on the sea coast of north-western Europe or not very far from it. Thence come the Boulonnais, Breton, Percheron, Fresian, Brabançon, Rhenish and the Mecklenburg.

The two remaining groups of horses, the

Mongolian steppe horse and the North European
" forest " horse, are the ones least influenced by
man. They are still to be found in the places
where they have existed since time was and they
would probably still exist, even if they were in a
wild state, almost unchanged now. While " cold-
blood " and " hot-blood " horses and the " warm-
blood " horse are usually bred in more or less
artificial conditions and under the strict supervision of man—who interferes in their breeding
increasingly, emphasising one or other of their
characteristics, such as speed and stamina in the
English Thoroughbred, weight and size as in
Boulonnais and Percheron—steppe horses are bred
in *kossiak*, which embraces about 20 mares and a
stallion. A number of *kossiaks* make a *taboon*,
which consists of hundreds of horses. In Russia
this *taboon* horse-breeding has been adopted on a
large scale. To increase the size and general
improvement of the steppe horse in certain
regions, every 20 Kirgiz or Don mares were given
an English Thoroughbred stallion and were
turned out on to the steppe, where they lived a
whole year round, being only sometimes provided
with hay in winter. Usually, however, they have
to look after themselves and pick up their food
sometimes from under the snow. Young stock
suffers still more privation if local *kozaks* are
milking mares to get the popular beverage known
as *kumys* (fermented milk).

The compromise between artificial horse-
breeding strictly under man's control and *taboon*
horse-breeding is the Hungarian system described
by Captain M. H. Hayes in his work " Points of
the Horse " :

In good Hungarian studs, the brood mares and their foals are kept in paddocks, and, if thought necessary, are housed at night. The yearlings, after the colts have been castrated, are turned out about March, with the two and three-year-olds, on the open *puszta* by the *csikos* (cowboys), who generally ride old barren mares and keep the animals together with their long whips. The young stock have to live off what they can find during their outing, which lasts till October, and they and their *csikos* have no artificial shelter. The man gets a weekly supply of bread, bacon and salt, but rarely a warm meal, except when he kills some game and roasts it for himself. The climate during summer and autumn in those parts is very hot and dry. In October the herd is driven home, housed at night, and kept in paddocks during the day. The *csikos* give a particular name to each youngster, who begins to recognise it in a remarkably short time. When housed, each colt and filly is tied up to the manger in one particular place and it soon learns to find its allotted spot. If it is not in its place, the *csikos* call out its name, and by flicks of the whip, drive it into its proper abode in a very short time. When they are all correctly placed, they are tied up and fed for the night, and in the morning are turned into the paddocks. This routine is observed until spring comes round. During this winter course, each of them gets hay and from 3 to 6 litres ($5\frac{1}{4}$ to $10\frac{1}{2}$ pints) of corn. Towards the end of the year, the three-year-olds are taken up, broken to saddle and harness, and are generally put aside for sale to dealers who visit these well-organised studs.

The North European type of horse not only resembles the type of steppe horse, but can also probably claim kindredship. The scientific researches of the twenty years before the Second World War were based mostly on comparison of the head and skeleton of the steppe horse and those of wild horses (*Equus caballus forma silvatica*) which lived in central and north-western Europe and claimed resemblance and consanguinity with the Polish ponies and those of the Scottish Highland. Both these latter breeds are derived, according to Ewart, from *Equus celticus*, thus proving that ancestors of both groups were steppe horses living in the basin of the Black Sea. Those which went to the north-west partly died out because of severe climatic conditions and difficulties of feeding, while some returned to the Black Sea basin, the remainder adapting themselves to new conditions of life which had a certain influence on their type.

According to local conditions, soil, climate and admixture of new blood with which they were crossed (Esthonian " Klepper," with a dash of Eastern blood) different breeds were established. All of them, however, retained many characteristics of the ancient wild forest horse, such as great hardiness, satisfaction with the poorest food, great strength for their size, prepotency and longevity. They are mostly dun-coloured with a black stripe through the back and black mane and tail, grey and dark.

The North European horse has many representatives in Europe, instanced by varieties of British ponies such as the Scottish Highland pony, Shetland, Finnish and Swedish ponies, Russian Viatka pony, Smudish, Polish lowland *mierzyn* and mountain pony (*hucul*).

Today Europe cannot be divided into regions where horses of uniform type live separately, but all above-mentioned types of horses may be found in almost every country living one beside the other.

AKHAL-TEKE

This is one of the most ancient and one of the most beautiful breeds in existence, and was evolved by the " Teke " and Turkoman tribe in the oases of southern Turkmeina. Owing to the arid desert conditions, these Akhal-Teke horses, from time immemorial, have been tethered and hand-fed with a mixture of lucerne and barley. They are specialised saddle-horses bred to exist under conditions of great heat and privation. Their conformations are elegant in the extreme, with beautiful Persian heads, a noble expressive eye, long fine necks, and the best of legs and feet. They might be termed the greyhound among horses, for their fine-drawn conformation points to a similar speed. Their colour is unique, for although bays and greys are known, the most desired is a pale honey-gold, with black points.

Many breeds of animals and birds produce from time to time pure white specimens, and the white or Albino horse, which is of course a colour type, not a breed, has since 1937 been fostered and developed in America by the American Albino Horse Club. The foundation sire is said to have been " Old King," foaled in 1906, with breeding unknown, though he is believed to have been of Arabian-Morgan stock. Although with very careful selection, particularly in regard to colour, any type of Albino horse can be developed, whether for riding or for draught, since " Old King " is regarded as the foundation sire, and as a great many Albino horses used for circuses and parades are descended from him, a short description is desirable.

This horse was 15·2 hands high and strongly built. No dark spots appeared on his skin, which was of the necessary pink colour, and his hair was snow-white and silky, both mane and tail being very full. Possessed of sound endurance and of a vigorous character, he had nevertheless a quiet disposition, his action was commanding and his intelligence considerable. He is further described as having had a short, heavily muscled back with a well-rounded, close-ribbed body, legs of flat bone and white hair around the hoofs.

Albino horses are bred for those to whom a white horse appeals, and many naturally are used for ceremonial purposes and in the circus ring. Such being the case, a large number of these horses have been taught the traditional acts of the performing horse, and the claim that the Albino is a horse of exceptional intelligence may well be based on this. That he is a beautiful horse is true enough, but it must be remembered that as a ceremonial or circus horse he is shown at his best and is exhibited in ideal surroundings and handled expertly—advantages which many other horses do not enjoy.

It is claimed of this line of Albino horses that the stock is very prepotent, particularly in regard to colour, and that even when crossed with coloured mares they produce many beautiful snow-white foals. If, as is supposed, " Old King " was of Arabian-Morgan stock, this prepotency can well be understood, for this is a marked characteristic of both those breeds.

BREED SOCIETY : The American Albino Horse Club.

An interesting example of breeding for a particular purpose is the American Quarter Horse. It began in Virginia in very early days, where, owing to the lack of cleared sites for proper racecourses, the first horse-racing in America was carried on along short improvised tracks called "race paths," which were in fact cut out of the virgin wilderness. These tracks were usually about a quarter of a mile long, and so the horse which was bred to race on these tracks was called the "Quarter Horse."

For this type of racing a very quick starter and fast sprinter was required, and in due course a specific type was produced, originally from a cross of Thoroughbred stallions and native mares. These latter were no doubt mostly of Spanish origin from stock brought in from Florida through the Carolinas, but some were of Thoroughbred blood.

From a genealogical point of view the Quarter Breed starts from an English Thoroughbred, "Janus," which flourished in Virginia and North Carolina between 1756 and 1780. His distance in England was actually four miles, but curiously enough his progeny in America were generally noted for their speed over short distances, and had few equals in quarter-racing. "Janus" stood 14·2 hands, and his outstanding physical characteristic was his heavy and powerful hind-quarters, with great, prominent muscles. The breed that he propagated still exists and is officially known as the American Quarter Horse.

The special points of these horses are closeness to the ground, tremendous power, heavy frames extremely well muscled up, especially in the hind-quarters, loin and back. The withers, it should be noted, are low. The height of stallions is usually about 15 hands, and weight nearly 1,200 lb. They have great speed from 200 yards to a quarter of a mile, which is their limit. They are much favoured by cattle men for the work of rounding up cattle, as their fast starting and sprinting enables them to head any beast quickly, and is combined with nimbleness and weight and strength which gives them power to hold a heavy steer when it is roped. In addition, they possess a calmness of temperament which is not affected by sudden starts and changes of speed, and they have the ability to do well on any kind of food.

BREED SOCIETY. American Quarter Horse Association.

AMERICAN SADDLE

This breed is a peculiarly transatlantic product, and one in which Americans take great pride. It emanates from the early pioneering days of the first settlement of the country 400 years ago, when there were only two means of movement across the vast distances of the new continent—water and horseback. There was no indigenous horse in America, so the early settlers, like the Spaniards, brought their own or imported them soon after. English amblers and pacers came out before the days of the Thoroughbred, together with horses from Spain, France, Africa and the East. All these went to make up the American Saddle Horse.

The pioneers had to have a light, strong, hardy, speedy animal, comfortable to ride over long distances, adaptable to harness, good-tempered and intelligent. Accordingly they bred, with careful selection, from the best stock available, including in due course the English Thoroughbred, which gave the breed its fire and brilliance ; while it inherited the gentleness and easy gaits of the older English amblers. Various other American stocks have been introduced in the course of time, Morgan, Standard Bred (which are both dealt with in this book) and so on ; but the officially designated founder of the present type is the Thoroughbred " Denmark " (foaled 1839). It is well to note, however, that the parent of the breed, the Kentucky Saddle Horse, was an established product before that time. The blood of " Messenger," the ancestor of the American trotter, also runs in this breed.

The points of the breed are as follows. Height 15 to 16 hands, preferably not more. In conformation it should be light and elegant, with a good head, long, fine neck, well-sloped shoulders, round barrel, flat croup and good clean legs. The general appearance must be one of breeding and brilliance, with high, proud carriage of head and tail and a stance that covers plenty of ground. In character it must be docile and intelligent.

The speciality of the breed is the gaits which it exhibits in the show-ring, for which it is now almost exclusively bred. These gaits are the usual walk, trot and canter, and also the artificial paces, the running walk, stepping pace or slow rack and the fast rack. Animals are specially trained in each gait, and are known as three- or five-gaited horses according to training. The trot must be highly collected, with the head well flexed, neck and tail arched. The action must be high and smooth and speedy. The rack is a single-footed pace, each foot coming down singly and with great speed, a steady 1-2-3-4 with no pauses, each beat being equal. The stepping pace is really a very old pace often seen in local animals in India and the East and in a good trotting camel, the feet on each side following each other instead of stepping diagonally as in the ordinary trot. These gaits performed with the grace and precision for which the breed is famed are a spectacle never to be forgotten.

The characteristic carriage of the tail is obtained by nicking the muscles of the dock and then setting it in position with a crupper.

With its dynamic action, its three or five gaits, not to mention the peculiar and unnatural set of its tail, this horse is unforgettable. And those that reach the highest standard in America present a horse in action comparable only with hackney horses and ponies. The breed can be found really nowhere outside America, nor is it likely ever to receive any measure of popularity were it brought to England, especially now that the law in this country prohibits the nicking and docking of horses' tails.

The American Saddle Horse, as the name implies, is of course used primarily for saddle work, but as the action of this horse is high and exaggerated in the extreme it is unlikely to find general favour anywhere else in the world where the smooth, low, long and level action is considered as the ideal.

BREED SOCIETY: American Saddle Horse Breeders Association.

ANGLO-ARAB

As the title implies, this is a composite breed, but it is so well established and so universally recognised as a breed that it is entitled to a place among the world's breeds of horses. It may be said too, that it has an especial claim to this, because it is composed of the two purest breeds, the Arab and the Thoroughbred, and possesses no alien blood.

The authority in England controlling the breed is the Arab Horse Society, which keeps a Stud Book or Register for the purpose, the conditions of entry being that the Anglo-Arab in question must be : (1) The produce only of Arab horses which are entered either in the Arab Horse Stud Book or the General Stud Book (Arabian Section), and of horses entered in the General Stud Book other than the Arabian Section of the same. (2) Horses directly descended from ancestors which are eligible for entry under the conditions set out at (1) above. (3) Anglo-Arabs bred in foreign countries and entered in the recognised stud books of those countries may also be accepted for registration, if approved by the Council of the Arab Horse Society.

The more usual breeding is by the Arab horse on the Thoroughbred mare, and whether this or the reverse breeding be the case, it can well be understood that the result is a horse of outstanding quality, always supposing that the sire and dam are typical specimens of their respective breeds. It is noticeable, however, that whereas one specimen will be strongly Arab, the other may be markedly Thoroughbred. In the same way as with all breeding, no certainty of height can be looked for, except that the resulting animal will probably be somewhere in height between its sire and dam.

In numberless breed and saddle classes Anglo-Arabs have figured with success in competition with most other breeds of light horses. Because of the added stamina and intelligence derived through the Arab, the Anglo-Arab has proved itself to be a good hunter and a very beautiful hack, having all the necessary gaiety and airiness of movement and the great refinement necessary for this class of animal. It has made its mark in flat-races, steeplechases and point-to-point races and in the show-ring, and it is naturally an excellent medium as a dressage horse.

A *description* of the breed must necessarily be an admixture of the parents. For these, reference is made to the descriptions of each breed, and it should be emphasised that the true Anglo-Arab is a combination of both, without displaying to a marked degree the outstanding characteristics of either. It is claimed for the breed that it should be the Thoroughbred at its best with rather more of the classic Arabian head, the vivid tail carriage and the added intelligence which is expected of and found almost invariably in the Arab.

In dealing with the Anglo-Arab it is as well to call attention to the fact that the Arab is very largely used as a cross to produce riding-horses and ponies in England. None of these represents a breed in itself, nor indeed hardly a type, but so very many good specimens are continually being produced that it is as well to record the fact. The breeds and types used for this are very many, ranging from Hunters to Shetland Ponies, of which perhaps one of the most popular is the Arab-Welsh cross, a pony having a number of virtues, and in particular enjoying a reputation of being perhaps the most beautiful pony in the country. The Arab has been crossed with varying success, but at times most satisfactorily, with some of the heavier breeds, good specimens having been produced by introducing Arab blood to the Suffolk and Percheron.

The Arab Horse Society of England is likely to establish in the future some ruling as to the minimum amount of Arab blood which will be permitted in the Anglo-Arab to justify registration in the Anglo-Arab Registry. It may be recorded that from time to time through the last century or so attempts have been made—and indeed are still being made—to reintroduce Arab blood into the English Thoroughbred and in so doing to produce a horse able to compete on equal terms with the Thoroughbred race-horse.

BREED SOCIETY (in England) : The Arab Horse Society.

ANGLO-NORMAN

In the origin of this breed we find, as the foundation, a Norman horse which was a powerful and enduring animal, and very much appreciated in those times as a war horse. William the Conqueror is said to have brought to England a large number of these horses, which did much good in improving the English native horse.

In later times the Norman horse deteriorated by careless crossing with the Danish and Mecklenburg cart-horse, and since 1775 Arabs and English Thoroughbreds and half-breds were used. Between 1834–60 a large admixture of Norfolk trotter blood gave origin to the Anglo-Norman trotter, which was chiefly bred in the district of Morleraut (Department of Orne). The soil of this district is rich in lime and iron, and in addition to this, qualities of water and climate favour the breeding of an excellent horse with good bone and strong muscles. Anglo-Norman trotters are very hardy and enduring and have a very good reputation.

Besides this group of trotters there are two main types of Anglo-Norman : first, the draught type, standing from 15·2 to 17 hands with a strong admixture of Percheron and later of Boulonnais blood, usually grey, but sometimes bay, chestnut or black. The horse was used as a mail-cart horse, thanks to a capacity of pulling a heavy load at a good trot. Secondly, there is the cavalry type, which is much used in the army and for sport. Although some of them are excellent horses there are many of them which do not answer military requirements and are an unhappy combination of two breeds. Being " well-topped," their hocks and bone below the knees are deficient, sometimes consisting of inharmonious pieces inherited from the Norman, others from the English Thoroughbred. Good ones, however, make really excellent horses for sport and military service. Those which are not sold to the army make a horse for general use.

While the heavier type was bred in the region of Mortagne, Anglo-Norman saddle horses were bred on a large scale around Caen.

Normandy is also a great breeding centre for racehorses, where in past days " Capucin " and many other prominent racehorses were bred, as was " Bois Roussel," winner of the 1938 English Derby.

APPALOOSA

The spotted horse, beloved of the circus and used frequently as the " drum " horse for mounted bands, is to be found in many different parts of the world. Of recent years commendable efforts have been made in the United States of America to establish and standardise the breed and the Appaloosa Horse Club has been formed there.

The name is derived, it seems, from a breed which was developed by the Nez Percé Indians in the Palouse country of Central Idaho and Eastern Washington, and was developed primarily for war uses. Something akin to these horses has been found in ancient Chinese paintings dating back over 3,000 years. A similar type of horse is also known as the Colorado Ranger, for which an authority claims that they are American-bred Moroccan Barbs derived from stock imported from Spanish Andalusia.

The body is pink-skinned and covered by a silky white coat with a large number of black spots superimposed. The spots are of varying sizes and it is a curious fact that they can be felt by a touch of the finger. They are found on all parts of the body and legs, and are in more profusion on the quarters. The effect is very striking and makes them in great demand for circus work. The colouring on many occasions varies both as to the skin and the spots, chocolate often being the colour of the latter.

An infusion of Arab blood has given the horse a touch of quality, and this is particularly noticeable in the refinement of head and gaiety of carriage, making it an animal of considerable attraction not only in appearance but as a riding horse.

In height the Appaloosa may be said to be from 14·2 to 15·2 hands, thus being a handy size for riding, and he weighs, perhaps, 800 to 1,000 lb. Of good shoulder and body, with strong legs having plenty of bone and a well-defined wither, a good specimen conforms to the standard required for riding, and it should be noted that some horses exceed the height given.

With such attractive and arresting colouring and markings added to the qualities already enumerated, it is perhaps a little surprising that so ancient a breed is not found in larger numbers. The answer may be that there is some uncertainty in producing a sufficient number of the necessary spots, and these evenly distributed.

BREED SOCIETIES : The Appaloosa Horse Club (of America) and British Spotted Horse Society.

ARAB

Of all the horse breeds of the world, the Arab is not only the oldest and the most beautiful, but has had more influence on other breeds than any, which is the surest tribute to its excellence. No record exists of the horse's origin, but drawings and carvings are in existence which prove that it lived many centuries before the Christian era, and actual named horses have been found dating back nearly 5,000 years.

The "father" of all oriental or hot-blooded horses, the Arab has always been known to the Arabs as "Kehilan," which in Arabic means "Thoroughbred," though the breed itself is divided into a number of strains. The purity of blood has been guarded fanatically through the ages by the Arabs in the desert. Any admixture of foreign blood would have been unthinkable, and the breed can therefore properly claim to be the purest of all equine races.

Possessed of qualities unequalled in other breeds, such as soundness of wind, freedom from leg trouble, extreme endurance and the ability to live a life full of privations, it is small wonder that the best of its kind is greatly cherished and that specimens have fetched fabulous prices. Small wonder, too, that almost every breed and cross-breed throughout the world has at one time or another received an infusion of Arab blood. It should be recorded that every registered English Thoroughbred has Arab blood in its veins (see Thoroughbred). Its prepotency is so vivid and persistent that even today Thoroughbreds are constantly being foaled possessed of the striking Arabian form and presence.

The breed's outstanding features are : a small horse—the stallions standing about 14·2 to 15 hands, with mares slightly smaller—of extremely graceful carriage and beautifully refined head, with tail carried high and gaily ; a horse of arresting and picturesque appearance, indeed, the very picture horse of all the equine race. It is unmistakable and renowned throughout the world. It is deeply regretted that in recent years the breeding of the Arabian Horse in the desert has ceased to a great extent, but a number of studs of these beautiful horses exist in many countries, and the best are to be found in England.

An abbreviated description is given by the Rt. Hon. Lady Wentworth, perhaps the greatest living authority on the breed :

Head, small and profile concave, tapering to a very small muzzle. *Eyes*, very large, brilliant and circular, and placed low in the skull. *Nostrils*, very flexible and capable of enormous expansion.

Jowl, very deep and wide. *Ears*, small and sharply cut, quick and pricked. *Neck*, arched and set into the jaws in an arched curve. *Withers*, not so high, but slope into a strong level *back*. *Chest*, broad and deep. *Body*, well-ribbed-up. *Quarters*, broad and level. *Tail*, set on a level with the back and carried high. *Legs*, with iron tendons, large strong *hocks*, big flat *knees*, springy *pasterns*, well-developed *thighs*. *Feet*, hard and round. *Action*, free and fast at all gaits.

Because of its inherent virtues and the increasing demand for the riding horse in England as distinct from the hunter of the last century, the Arab in England has during the last 30 or 40 years increased enormously in popularity ; and although the trend of supply and demand varies from time to time, as it always must with any commodity, there is no doubt that the Arab, whether for reproducing the pure breed or for developing the Anglo-Arab or part-bred Arab, will continue to flourish.

This increased demand for the breed is perhaps all the more remarkable because the demand for any horse for army purposes is now practically non-existent. Prior to the 1914 war there was a strong demand for the export of Arab stallions from England to many parts of the world for army purposes, and it would seem now that the demand shows that the Arab has found an entirely new market and thrives there.

BREED SOCIETY : Arab Horse Society (of England).

45

ARDENNES

Ardennes may be considered either as a French or Belgian breed, as the mountains from which he originally came belong according to their exact location to either country.

The Ardennes is a very hardy horse, the most resistant of all to unfavourable conditions of climate and feeding. The breed is very old, and in the last three centuries submitted to many changes, such as increase in size and weight by crossing with Brabançons, which was done at the expense of other qualities of the breed, such as power of endurance, vigour and a very good action.

During the 17th century the Ardennes was used as a cavalry horse by Marshal Turenne, and being a good stayer, very hardy, docile, but with a lively temperament, he was much appreciated. During Napoleon's campaign against Russia in 1812 Ardennes distinguished themselves, enduring all the hardships much better than other breeds. So did they during the First World War, but then served more as artillery wheelers, as by this time their type was already changed again. Today there exists in the mountains a small Ardennes from 14·2 to 15·1 hands, which is nearest to the old original type, while others are of heavy draught type. The horse is very popular not only in France and Belgium but also in other countries, and in Sweden Ardennes form as much as 60 per cent. of all the horse population.

Now that the transport in towns and work on farms has become so greatly mechanised, the future of this famous Ardennes breed must, with that of so many others, be largely problematical. But where a working horse of low draught and great hardiness is required, combined with a good free moving gait, the breeding of the Ardennes will continue. No longer, of course, will this horse be required for army purposes and it is likely that more and more will it be found only in its own country.

ASS (or DONKEY)

The domesticated ass, or donkey, with his friendly but self-willed disposition, is a familiar enough sight all over the world, and does not need a long or detailed description. There are local variations, but generally he is a slatey grey in colour, averaging 10 to 11 hands in height, with a thick, coarse coat, big head, flat withers, little box-like feet and black dorsal and shoulder stripes. These, forming a cross on his back, are traditionally supposed to date from that first Palm Sunday when he carried Our Lord into Jerusalem. He is proverbially—and actually—very long-lived, a dead donkey being, according to Pickwickian Sam Weller, one of the two things that " no man ever see " ; the other being a dead post-boy! In country lore the braying of a donkey is said to presage rain or hail—" It is time to cock your hay and corn, when the old donkey blows his horn."

In many countries, the East especially, the donkey seems to be permanently associated with the laundry trade, and can be seen carrying enormous bundles of clothes and often a man on top of them into the bargain. In India there are two types of domesticated donkey, the small grey and the large white. The small grey averages 8 hands in height, and in colour is the usual dark grey with black markings ; the large white averages about 11 hands and is almost white in colour.

The Wild Ass is found in two distinct types in Africa and Asia respectively. The African animal, which is the stock from which the domesticated breeds are derived, inhabits Nubia, Eastern Sudan and Somaliland, and is very rare. He has large ears and small narrow hoofs, and his voice is the familiar bray. In colour he is grey with a white belly. Fast and sure-footed and much larger than the domesticated " Neddy," he lives in small herds in remote desert tracts.

The Wild Ass of Asia is more horse-like than the African, has smaller ears and is sandy or dun in colour instead of slate grey. His voice is a sort of stifled bray, described by R. I. Pocock as " a squealing inhalation after a guttural exclamation."

One distinct variety, the Kiang, is found in the highlands of Tibet up to altitudes of 16,000 feet. Apart from the general sandy or light chestnut colour, the dorsal stripe and tail tuft are black, while the muzzle, under neck, belly, legs, and backs of thighs are creamy-white. The colour becomes darker in the winter, when the coat is long and thick. The Kiang is a powerfully built animal ranging in height from 12 to 13 hands, lives in small herds, is very fast for his size and an exceptionally strong swimmer, plunging unhesitatingly into the most turbulent and icy mountain torrents.

Various local races of Asian Wild Ass, rather smaller and more lightly built than the Kiang, are found in the desert regions of North-west India, Persia (onager), Tartary and Mongolia (dziggetai). The local race of Syria, which must have been the often-mentioned wild ass of the Bible, is now extinct.

Great numbers of donkeys of a particularly loveable type have always been bred in Ireland, where the " ass cart " is a familiar sight.

It is a notable fact that, so placid is the donkey by nature, and so friendly in its approach to horses, that it is often turned out with them at grass to exercise a calming influence. In this it is invariably successful.

AUSTRALIAN (Waler)

There are few more famous horses in the British Empire than the Waler, the national horse of Australia, though he is not often seen in England. The term "Waler" is a comprehensive national term covering a variety of types, and an abbreviation of New South Wales, the state where the Australian horse was first imported and bred.

There was no indigenous native horse in Australia, and the first arrivals from the outer world came in 1795, from the Cape and Chile. So the foundation stock of the Waler was of Dutch and Spanish origin, with the oriental horses the Arab and the Barb as the ultimate ancestors. (See also the note on the Cape Horse under Basuto.)

These original animals were small, and as the settlers had great need for riding horses and

50

wanted the best, pure Arabs and English Thoroughbreds were imported. The country, with its equable climate, unlimited range, and wide choice of pasturage, was eminently suitable for horse-breeding, which was carried out with great care ; and the Australian Horse developed and flourished. It has been asserted, with some justification, that between Waterloo and the Crimea Australia possessed probably the best saddle horse in the world, and during that period began the supply of cavalry and artillery troop horses to India. Racing, which first appeared in Australia in 1826, further helped to establish the Australian Horse, the breeding of which has spread in the natural course of time from New South Wales to the states of Victoria and Queensland ; but the name " Waler " still applies to them all.

The discovery of gold in 1851 very nearly ruined the Waler. The wholesale desertion of the ranges for the goldfields led to the neglect of the stock, which strayed and became half wild, breeding indiscriminately and haphazardly, with the result that the breed seriously deteriorated ; nor did the admixture of cart-horse blood which took place about that time tend to help the saddle horse. By 1880 New South Wales was overstocked with underbred and valueless horses, from which state of affairs it took a long time to recover. However, by one of those famous whirligigs of time, the gold plutocrats found racing and horses good things to spend their money on, and interest in both revived, though the resuscitation of the stock was retarded by the popularity of short sprint races and by racing the youngsters too soon. Still, the revival did take place, especially during this century.

Export to India continued on a large scale up to the age of mechanisation, with a variety of animals : coarse, strong gunner " hairies," thoroughbreds for breeding and racing, cavalry horses, polo ponies, some of which were really beautiful compact little animals unequalled anywhere.

The Waler has always been noted for jumping in his own country, high-jumping competitions being a speciality at all shows. The world's highest ridden jump, 8 feet 4 inches, was made by a Waler in 1940. Another speciality at which he can at times excel is buckjumping, equalling in this respect, in the opinion of many, that better-known exponent the American broncho. By the same token the Australian range rider takes his place among the world's finest horsemen.

Australian horses are all shapes and sizes, including besides the Waler a draught-horse breed developed from three English strains—Clydesdale, Shire, and Suffolk Punch—and the ponies of Western Australia, from stock brought from Timor. This Timor stock must have been representative of the Java horse from the islands of Java and Sumatra.

Times have changed in the horse world so very greatly since the period during the wars that the Waler as a breed will become increasingly less known and, so far as the world outside Australia is concerned, the breed will probably become extinct. This is a great pity in view of the qualities we have described of this outstanding horse.

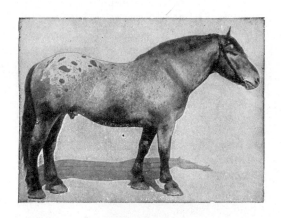

In Austro-Hungary before the war, besides indigenous and a large number of of half-bred horses used for both saddle and harness, there were Austrian breeds such as the Lippizana, Kladruber and Pinzgauer. The Kladruber horse takes its name from a place in Bohemia where it was bred at the Imperial Stud. They are derived from Spanish horses imported to Austria and Bohemia from Spain and Italy, and from which they inherited most of their typical characteristics, such as conformation, high action, roman noses, long, heavy-crested arched necks. The selection went in the direction of increasing considerably their size (they stand 17 to 18 hands) and producing either black or white animals. With their high action in teams of six or eight of one colour they made the most imposing Imperial carriage horses and were used only on very big occasions. Their practical value was never taken into much account.

The Pinzgauer, usually roan in colour, is a very powerful, heavy-draught horse standing 15 to 16 hands, and having clean, strong legs. It is said to trace its origin to the Friesian horses and was bred first in the Pinzgau district of Styria. Later on its breeding was extended to Upper Austria and its export organised.

As will be seen from the illustration, the Pinzgauer is a typical heavy-draught horse of good shape, having an exceptionally good body and satisfactory shoulder for the work required of it. Short on the leg, it is admirably suited for low, heavy, direct traction, and as the Percheron is to France, so was the Pinzgauer to Austria. Its future, as with that of other horses required for work as distinct from pleasure, must be problematical. Being of the Percheron and Suffolk type, with its " clean " or " hairless " fetlocks and lower limbs, the breed may be counted upon to enjoy some of the virtues of these two, but if anything it lacks the lightness of movement which is always claimed for the Suffolk.

As with all breeds of heavy or cold-blood horses, what these typical Austrian horses lack in activity and intelligence they gain in tractability and docility. Having regard to their great strength— and this again applies to all heavy breeds—those who handle them can only be thankful for this placid temperament.

BALEARIC

Another ancient breed is to be found in the island of Majorca, in the Balearic group. These horses, which are most abundant in the Palma district, differ markedly from all other breeds. Especially characterised by their slender limbs and free, graceful carriage, they vary in colour from dark to light brown, and have short, thick and arched necks, with thick, upright manes, which are often clipped.

The delicate head, with backwardly directed ears, is distinctly roman-nosed, and, when the animal is galloping, is carried sharply bent against the short neck. In this respect the Majorca breed differs markedly from Algerian and Andalusian horses, which carry their heads stretched out straight, nearly in the line of the neck. The Majorca horses may be compared to those depicted on ancient vases and Greek coins, and it is believed that they are the survivors of the ancient type.

This identification, if trustworthy, is of great interest, as it serves to indicate that the hog-manes of the early Grecian horses, like those sculptured on the frieze of the Parthenon, were natural, although, as in the case of the Majorca breed, improved by trimming. This seems to be indicative of the affinity of both breeds to the wild tarpan ; and affords further evidence that the falling manes of modern horses (other than the Arab) are due to domestication.

From the above it will be appreciated that the Balearic breed is, from the point of view of the student of horse-breeding, one of exceptional interest, and even the novice on reading this short description will realise that this is a most unusual breed.

This breed had its native home in Morocco and Algeria, and in its original form stood from 14 to 15 hands in height. It is characterised by flat shoulders, rounded chest, relatively long head, and, as compared with the Arab, the lower setting of the tail, the hair of which, like that of the mane, is profusely developed. The prevailing colours are dark bay, brown, chestnut, black and grey. The skull has the same sinuous profile as that of the Arab. Formerly the Barb was extensively crossed with Syrian Arabs, while later in Algeria it was much mingled with European horses, so that pure-bred animals became very far from easy to obtain. The Barb will thrive on as poor fare as the Arab and is equally hardy in constitution and docile in temper, although somewhat less spirited. Several strains of the Barb type were recognised by Colonel Hamilton Smith, the first of which was reared by the Mograbins on the western side of the plains south of the Atlas, to whom it was known as " Shrubat-ur-rich " (Drinker of the Wind). These horses, which were either grey or brown in colour, were low and greyhound-like in shape, and carried very little flesh. More remarkable is the Bornu breed, from the district south of Lake Chad, which is greyish-white in colour with black legs. The tail is set rather low, the legs and feet are beautifully made and the body is relatively short.

A third breed occurs typically in the Dongola district of Nubia, but is also found in Alfaia and Gerri. Typical horses of this breed are very similar in make to the Bornu type, but those of Alfaia and Gerri are smaller.

Although single specimens are found from time to time, the Barb has for many years now been practically non-existent in England. This is a pity, for there is much that is good about the breed, and its reputation for hardiness is unsurpassed. Its absence is particularly to be regretted as it is essentially a riding-horse, and it is, after all, the riding-horse that will survive in numbers. The reason for its lack of popularity in this country is possibly that it cannot compete in favour with the other great oriental breed, the Arab.

This, however, can be no excuse for the virtual eclipse of the breed outside its native land, for a good Barb would always compare favourably with many breeds of riding-horses and even surpass some of them.

The famous Basuto pony is not in its origin an indigenous African breed. The horse (*Equus caballus*) was unknown in South Africa until the middle of the 17th century, although his ultimate ancestor was flourishing on the North African littoral. With the enormous jungles that lay between the north and the south and the belts of the dreaded tsetse fly, there was little chance of him migrating southwards by land. The opening of the sea routes to the East by the Portuguese and Dutch prepared the way, and in 1653 four horses of Arab and Barb blood from Java were landed in the Cape by the Dutch East India Company. These were the first horses to set foot in South Africa, and they became the foundation of the Cape Horse, which was the direct ancestor of the Basuto Pony.

The importation of oriental strains—Arab,

Barb and Persian—continued steadily up to 1811. In the 18th century, when the English began to be interested in the country, the introduction of English Thoroughbred stock began. Between 1770 and 1790 especially, many good English stallions were imported, mainly descendants of " Herod," " Matcham," and " Eclipse," so the Byerley Turk, and Darley and Godolphin Arabians were all represented, and the oriental ancestry was present on both sides.

The Cape Horse breed flourished during the early years of the 19th century, figured conspicuously in the Boer War and achieved a high reputation for looks and stamina. Then, partly owing to lack of interest and the introduction of inferior foreign stock, the quality of the breed dropped off, and has deteriorated considerably since 1860, and is now for all practical purposes represented by the Basuto.

The Cape Horse was introduced into Basutoland as a result of border raids and the confusion caused by the invasion of that territory by the Zulus from 1822 onwards. The stolen horses figured in many a conflict, contributing great moral effect on behalf of those who had ventured to ride them. From about 1830 onwards the type developed into the Basuto pony as he is known today : small, thickset, short legs, longish back, very hard hoofs, with that bit of quality about the head which declares his high ancestry. Brought up and worked among the formidable heights of the Drakensberg with no horsemastership or care, but ridden by absolutely fearless riders, the Basuto became as tough and self-reliant as a wild horse and one of the most fearless and surefooted ponies in the world, being habitually ridden at a gallop up and down hills where most other horses and riders would hesitate to walk. The endurance of these ponies, too, is very great, and they are capable of carrying 13 or 14 stone for 60 to 80 miles a day. In their own country they became in great demand for racing and polo.

Although Basutos were much used in the Boer War, the breed had already begun to decline, the descent becoming more rapid in the beginning of this century. Efforts were then started, and are now continuing, to revive the breed by the introduction of good Arab stallions and carrying out breeding on systematic lines. The experiment of introducing Highland Pony blood was tried in 1917, but the cross was not ultimately successful.

In a country such as South Africa where records seem to show that an increased interest is being taken in the breeding of light horses, where polo flourishes in a smallish way and where riding clubs and pony clubs increase in numbers, the Basuto pony may well stage a come-back. It may be that the pony will be crossed to the extinction of the true Basuto, but the latter gained for itself such a world-wide reputation for hardiness, sure-footedness and ability to thrive on the smallest fare that there are strong hopes that it may survive as a breed where others may unhappily proceed to extinction.

The solution—if indeed there is a solution—must of course lie in the answer to the question as to whether there is a sufficient demand for a specified and controlled breeding of a riding pony for work or pleasure in South Africa. If there is, then it is to be hoped that such efforts will be concentrated on the Basuto Pony.

BATAK or DELI

Akin to the Manipuris are the Batak or Deli ponies of Sumatra, which were bred in the Batak hills of that island and were exported to Singapore from the port of Deli in large numbers. With their handsome, high-bred-looking heads and high-crested necks, they differ, however, markedly from the Mongolian and Yarkandi types, which are often more or less decidedly ewe-necked; this difference being due to a strong infusion of Arab blood. In stature they average only about 11·3 hands, although some reach 12·1 or 12·2 hands. Although most are brown, skewbalds are by no means uncommon. Sumatra also possesses a second breed of ponies, which take their name from the Gayoe hills, at the northern end of the island.

BEBERBECK

The Beberbeck Horse originates from the Beberbeck region in Germany, which was chosen for a stud because of its excellent natural conditions favouring horse-breeding. The Beberbeck Stud was founded more than a hundred years ago and existed until several years after the First World War, when the whole stud was bought by the Polish Government. When one looks in the pedigree of the Beberbeck horse one finds that in its roots there were local mares improved by Arab stallions. Then the systematic crossing with English Thoroughbred stallions took place. In breeding Beberbeck horses, however, one principle was strictly observed, namely, that the mare got by an English Thoroughbred stallion was never covered by an English Thoroughbred stallion again, but by a home-bred Beberbeck stallion. Finally, Beberbeck horses represented a heavier type of the English Thoroughbred, with a very good conformation, deep in the girth and with a lot of bone. Their adversaries alleged that they were inclined to softness, but a test organised in Poland for half-bred horses proved that the Beberbecks were a very good type of cavalry horse, and very useful for agricultural work, also making good light cart-horses. They stand usually over 16 hands, their colour in general being bay and chestnut.

From post-war information it seems that, for practical purposes, this breed has ceased to exist.

BEETEWK

Amongst several foreign breeds of heavy-draught horses introduced into Russia, such as Brabançon, Ardennes, Vladimir Clydesdale, which are of complex hybrid origin and to the formation of which Clydesdales, Dutch, Danish, Suffolk and other " cold-blood " breeds have contributed, there is a Russian original heavy-draught breed known as Beetewk. Its name is derived from the Beetewk River (Veronej Province), on the banks of which the breed was founded. Local mares, being of quite good quality, attracted the attention of Peter the Great in the beginning of the 18th century, and he was responsible for breeding these mares to imported Dutch stallions, while the results of those matings were crossed with Orlov Trotters, hence the great ability in some of them for trotting, which makes them also good coaching horses. Although the breed diminished in size when the rich pastures of their breeding region were turned into arable land, they still stand over 16 hands and are strong enough to pull over three tons. Their strength, endurance, good action and high spirits, combined with great obedience and docility, make them very valuable agricultural horses, and no foreign breed of heavy type can compete against them under Russian conditions.

BOULONNAIS

The early history of the Boulonnais (French) breed is of a horse which was bred in that region during the Crusades and was much improved by Arab and Barb stallions brought from the Middle East by the French Crusaders. In the course of ages this breed submitted to certain changes and at one time, before railways were popularised. the Boulonnais existed in the form of a very strong horse with good action and stamina, which enabled it to be used in coaches for fast transport, such as bringing fresh oysters from the sea coast to Paris.

The type enjoyed great fame and was exported to other countries where a strong, fast-moving carriage horse, having endurance, was needed. Some of them were exported before the First World War to Poland, and they appeared to be very useful when crossed with local stock, probably thanks to the link of Arab blood which at one time was introduced into both breeds.

Today the Boulonnais is a very heavy-draught horse, standing 16 to 17 hands, quick-growing, with great bone and muscles, and may be used for farm work when it is 18 months old. At 4–5 years old, being horses of enormous weight and power, they are usually employed in industry in big cities. The Boulonnais are much better movers than would be supposed. They are black, bay, red roan, blue roan and dappled grey. Once a type of " postier " and later an agricultural horse, Boulonnais today, through selection and very strong feeding, is a heavy-draught horse and is bred in two types : the Abbeville type, which is of medium size, and a large, very heavy Dunkirk type. Although their name derives from Boulogne, they are bred also in Picardy, Artois, Haute Normandy, and in parts of Flanders, where a strong, massive horse is needed for very heavy work.

Among connoisseurs of heavy-draught breeds the opinion prevails that a dash of Boulonnais blood in " cold-blood " breeds plays the same role as that of the English Thoroughbred in the breeding of saddle horses.

In the Boulonnais France has, with the Dutch Draught (q.v.), the strongest and most impressive draught horse in Europe. It resembles the Percheron (q.v.), not only in type but also largely in colour. The infusion of Arab blood in years gone by is still noticeable in many specimens of the breed, which for the same reason is claimed to possess a certain elegance in spite of its massive appearance.

BRABANÇON

Low-lying areas of Belgium with fertile soil and succulent herbage produced a large, very heavy-draught horse, with great power of traction. Brabançon, as it is called, stands between 16 and 17 hands and has great weight, which increases its tractive ability. It has a very good temperament and is a willing worker, which, together with a strong constitution, makes it popular abroad. It was used to a great extent for crossing with the Rhenish horse, while those imported to England had a certain influence on forming the

Shire breed. Brabançons are also bred in Russia, in the Gorki province, as pure or grade stock, and some of them are registered in state or district stud books.

Brabançons were also used for crossing with the old Belgian mountain breed of Ardennes to increase their size and weight.

Belgium, Holland and the northern parts of France have always been famous for producing heavy draught horses of real worth, so much indeed that their export has always been a very considerable trade. It is small wonder therefore that the Brabançon, with its 16 to 17 hands, its great weight and enormous strength, has not only always found a ready market in many parts, but has also proved invaluable for crossing.

When considering the origin of any heavy draught horse from any Continental country, with which is included England, it may be assumed that in many cases there has been a considerable admixture of the blood of various breeds. Bearing this in mind, it is interesting to note that in spite of this, the breeds themselves, whatever they may be, whether Shire, Clydesdale, Percheron, Ardennes or Brabançon, retain the characteristics of the breed itself.

The future of all cold-blood breeds is now in the balance. Their future must be a question of haulage economics, with which is involved the willingness or otherwise of labour to work the hours demanded by the keeping of horses—in short, week-end feeding.

BRETON

A breed which enjoys in France an excellent reputation, thanks to its great hardiness and working qualities, is the Breton. Bred on the rather poor land of Bretagne and exposed to a very rough climate, especially during winter, the Breton makes a very good agricultural horse, being strong and hardy and thriving on poor, indifferent food. There are three distinctive types of Breton horse : Breton heavy-draught horse, Breton draught post horse and Breton mountain draught horse.

The first one is bred on the fertile pastures near the sea coast and represents a type of heavy cart-horse. Those bred in the district of St. Pol de Léon, Côtes du Nord and Finistère stand from 15·2 to 16·2 hands, while the variety of Conquet bred in the south-east of Brest, is about 15·2 hands. They are strong and massive, standing on short legs protected by some feather, and are usually grey or bay.

In the interior of Bretagne there is bred a lighter horse, so-called draught post horse, which according to A. Magneville (" Carnet de Notes," N 2, 1944) is descended from the Norfolk Breton post horse. He stands about 15 to 16 hands, and being not only a strong and hardy horse but also a very good mover, makes a very valuable horse for the farmer.

Besides these two types, there exists a thick-set mountain draught Breton horse which is up to 14·3 hands, and is bred and employed in the mountainous part of Bretagne.

As is shown, the Breton horse is to be found in three types which in the main consist of animals of three different sizes—an example, of course, of a country or district breeding the type or types of horses which local requirements demand. This is comparable to the three types or sizes of the Highland pony in Scotland or those three to be found in Wales, the Cob, the Welsh pony of riding type, and the Welsh Mountain pony. The continued existence of the Breton as three types, or indeed its existence at all, must depend upon supply and demand, and it may well be that the smaller or mountain draught horse will be the one which survives.

In most of the countries lying to the eastward of the Bay of Bengal, including Burma, Annam, Thailand, the Malay Peninsula and Islands, the Liu Kiu Islands and a large portion of China, the horse is represented only by small breeds which come under the designation of ponies. Among these, the Burmese or Shan ponies, which are mainly, if not exclusively, bred by the hill-tribes of the Shan States, in the interior of the country, are believed to be nearly related to the Mongolian breed, although probably modified by the infusion of foreign blood. In stature they are about the equal of the Mongolian and are strong and active, although somewhat slow in their movements. On the other hand, the still smaller but closely allied Manipur (*q.v.*) ponies are much faster, and are used by their owners for polo, of which game Manipur is one of the original homes.

CLEVELAND BAY

Claimed as the oldest " established " breed of English horses, the Cleveland Bay is said to be possessed to an unrivalled extent of the power to transmit to any other breed with which it may be crossed those qualities for which all breeders look, namely, stamina, substance, action, wear and tear with style, appearance and good colour.

The chief use of this horse today is for mating with the Thoroughbred to obtain hunters of quality, up to weight and of good conformation, and for this purpose it is admirably suited. For a long time past it has been exported with great success, chiefly to America and the Colonies, to grade up to those qualities to which reference has been made horses of inferior breeding.

The breed is of great antiquity and its origin is uncertain, but it may be taken for granted that for a long period of time, in that district of Northern England, and chiefly in the county of Yorkshire, the breed is indigenous. More than a hundred years ago the Cleveland must have been the nearest to a fixed type of any race of horses in England, but none the less there were, even then, two types of Cleveland, the one used for agriculture and the other for coaching. It was claimed for the former, and indeed is so still, that it would do all the work of the heavier breeds, that it had the advantage over the Shires and the Clydesdales of being a clean-legged horse (that is, of course, that its heels are devoid of hair), and that it did the work more quickly, being very active-legged. For people in England and other countries it has served well as a ceremonial carriage horse in processions and other displays, and it has always been famous as a coach horse. The whole bay colouring, as the name implies, was suitable and attractive. A team of these bays to a road coach, with their level, striding action, is a sight which must be appreciated by all judges of a good horse.

A general description of the Cleveland Bay is :

Height, 15.3 to 16 hands, on short legs. *Colour*, bay to bay brown, with only a small white star permissible and a few grey hairs in heels and coronets. *Body*, wide and deep and not too long, but strong, with muscular loins. *Quarters*, level, powerful, long and oval, with tail springing well away from them. *Head*, rather large but well carried on a rather long, lean neck. *Limbs*, strong and muscular with knees and hocks well closed, having not less than nine inches of bone below the knee, and the legs should be clean of superfluous hair, with sloping pasterns.

BREED SOCIETY : The Cleveland Bay Horse Society.

CLYDESDALE

The history of the breed of Clydesdale Horses dates from the middle of the 18th century, when the hardy native breed found in Lanarkshire (Clydesdale being the old name for Lanarkshire) was being graded up to produce greater weight and substance by the use of imported Flemish stallions. The evolution of the breed was the direct result of the efforts of farmers of the Upper Ward of Lanarkshire to meet the demands of commerce, when, following the rapid developments of the surrounding coalfields causing road surfaces to be improved, shoulder haulage was substituted for pack-carrying.

The numbers of the Clydesdale breed seem to have been fairly progressive throughout the period, and in 1877 the Clydesdale Horse Society was formed and almost immediately published its first Stud Book. Since that first publication a very large number of stallions and mares have been registered. The breed has, beyond doubt, proved itself to be very popular and its adherents boast of the great numbers that have been exported as clear evidence of this. Quite spectacular prices have been obtained for big winners in the show ring and for export.

The outstanding characteristics of the Clydesdale are a combination of weight, size and activity, and what is looked for first and last by a Clydesdale man is exceptional wearing qualities of feet and limbs. The former must be round and open with hoof heads wide and springy, for any suspicion of contraction might lead to sidebones or ringbones. To some extent the further requirements of this breed vary somewhat from the orthodox and should be noted. The horse must have action, but not exaggerated, the inside of every shoe being made visible to anyone walking behind. The fore-legs must be well under the shoulders, not carried bull-dog fashion—the legs, in fact, must hang straight from shoulder to fetlock joint with no openness at the knee, yet with no inclination to knock. The hind legs must be similar, with the points of the hocks turned inwards rather than outwards, and the pasterns must be long.

The head must have an open forehead, broad across the eyes, the front of the face must be flat, neither dished nor roman, wide muzzle, large nostrils and a bright, clear, intelligent eye. A well-arched and long neck must spring out of an oblique shoulder with high withers ; the back should be short with well-sprung ribs ; and, as befits a draught horse, the thighs must be packed with muscle and sinew. The colour is bay, brown or black, with much white on face and legs, often running into the body, and it should be noted that chestnuts are rarely seen.

It is interesting to note that of the heavy breeds of horses in the British Isles, any white is strictly forbidden in the Suffolk, is obviously permitted in the case of the gay Percheron, allowed though contested in the Shire, whilst in the Clydesdale it is splashed about in most generous fashion. White-legged horses are never particularly favoured by the conscientious groom.

It is claimed of the Clydesdales that they are possessed of quality and weight without displaying grossness and bulk, and this is largely true. They are certainly active movers for their size and weight and in consequence are very popular in many cities and on numerous farms, especially in the north of England.

What the future of this breed as an agricultural horse may be is entirely problematical. From time to time those concerned in the breeding of agricultural horses are heartened by statements to the effect that farms are over-mechanised and that prosperity will return to the breeder of agricultural horses and indeed of horses required for town work. But it is only fair to say that no particular evidence of this suggested trend is shown. The Clydesdale in spite of its great size and consequent weight shows perhaps as much quality as, or even more than, any of the heavy breeds and to the lover of the draught horse its extinction would bring great sorrow.

BREED SOCIETY : The Clydesdale Society.

COB (Riding)

As with the hunter and the hack, and, indeed, with certain other well-known English representatives of the horse world, the Riding Cob is not a breed in itself. That it is a type and a well-known one is very certain, and for this reason no work covering the horses and ponies of the world would be complete without a reference, and a fairly full one at that, to this old-fashioned and still most popular horse.

It will be found that in the majority of the breeds mentioned in this book, other than the pure breeds or horses and ponies indigenous to any particular part of the world, it has been possible to indicate with a fair degree of certainty the components of the particular animal dealt with. This, however, is not even remotely possible in the case of the cob as a type, though, of course, the reverse is so often the case with the individual animal. It is indeed to a considerable extent a chance-bred animal, as will be readily concluded when its general appearance is considered.

The cob may be pictured briefly as a big-bodied, short-legged " stuffy " horse or pony standing no higher than 15·2 hands, with a small quality head set on a neck arched and elegant. The shoulders are laid obliquely, the back is short and the girth very great. The quarters generous to a degree and which, when viewed from behind, exceed expectations, having second thighs to match. The tail must be carried high, with gaiety, as befits a riding-horse. The action must be close to the ground, not rounded as with the harness horse, and the toe when in action must point to the farthermost limit—to an extent not exceeded, perhaps, in other breeds. The cannon bone should be extremely short.

Cobs are intended primarily for use as hacks, usually heavy-weight hacks for the more elderly rider, and for whatever the purpose, the riding cob must compare favourably, so far as manners are concerned, with that paragon of equine comportment, the hack. It is indeed the ideal ride for the elderly and portly, and is called upon to respect in manners and deportment the not-so-very-young.

If it were possible to fix a general line of original breeding no doubt the foundation of many of the best riding cobs has been that from which the Welsh Cob emanated, but equally it is beyond question that many outstandingly successful show-ring cobs have claimed close relationship to

77

half-bred cart mares and heavy-weight hunter mares put to stallions of quality. Whatever the forbears may have been, it is certain that there is nothing more typical nor more easy to recognise than the true Riding Cob. He leaves an unforgettable picture stamped upon the mind.

The Riding Cob has always been popular as a hunter (his great quarters make him outstanding as a performer over fences), as a horse to ride around the farm and as a trainer's hack because of his docility and manners.

The typical cob of the past, as the illustration shows, has always been docked, that is to say the tail has been cut to a length which so-called fashion dictated. Docking, as is known, has been prohibited in various countries for some long while past, and this rule now applies to England, and the prohibition extends to " nicking," which is another form of mutilation of the tail.

With or without the full tail, the cob of course remains, and will remain, as a horse up to a very great deal of weight, and his manner must be beyond reproach ; it will always be in demand as a riding horse for the more elderly, especially the smaller type which makes mounting easier for the not too agile. With its heavy body and short legs, big barrel and depth through the quarters, there is always a tendency for the cob to be heavy or jarring in its paces, and any suggestion of this of course detracts from its worth as a riding horse, especially for the elderly. Whether the cob of the show ring always conforms to the ideal is a matter of question, and may to some extent be judged by the onlooker. It might be mentioned that a class for cobs at shows is essentially an English institution.

BREED SOCIETY : The British Hack and Cob Association.

CONNEMARA

The term Connemara is applied to the breed
of pony which is found in that part of Connaught
in Ireland lying to the west of Loughs Corrib and
Mask, bounded on the west by the Atlantic and
on the south by Galway Bay. This area, which
is larger than the actual district of Connemara,
has been the home for centuries of an indigenous
primitive pony type, which until comparatively
recent years was left to fend for itself in an almost
feral state in wild and hard conditions.

In 1900 a Commission on Horse Breeding in
Ireland was set up, and Professor J. Cossor
Ewart, M.D., F.R.S., made a report after a very
thorough survey of the conditions and possi-
bilities of the Connemara pony. In 1928 the
present Connemara Pony Breeders' Society was
formed for the preservation and improvement of
the Connemara pony. At its first meeting the

Society decided on the policy of maintaining the breed intact by careful breeding from selected Connemara mares and stallions, so as to form a solid foundation stock. The original practice of crossing Connemara mares with stallions of other breeds was discontinued. This policy has been adhered to, and its results are to be found in the increasing uniformity with recognised standards, the better quality generally of mares—owing to the greater attention being paid to this by local breeders—and a decrease in the number of unlicensed stallions at large on mountain commonages and consequently less uncontrolled breeding; while the stamina of the breed, for which it has always been renowned, has not been affected.

Like all these representatives of the various primitive pony breeds of Europe, the origin of the Connemara is lost in the mists of history. It has been said that they owe their origin to horses saved from the wreck of the Spanish Armada in 1588, but it is more probable that the stock was present before that date. It has been suggested that with the Highland, the Shetland, the Iceland, and the Norwegian ponies (q.v.), it forms a Celtic pony type, with the wild horse of Mongolia as its remote ancestor, and also the addition of oriental strains at various times. The breed together with its primitive characteristics certainly shows signs of the admixture of Spanish and Arab blood, and might well have received the former in the times when the merchants of Galway traded regularly with Spain. However that may be, there seems no doubt that the Connemara pony is among the oldest inhabitants of the British Isles, and is a link with a very remote past.

The points and characteristics of the Connemara pony as defined in the Stud Book are as follows : Hardiness of constitution, staying power, docility, intelligence and soundness. *Height*, 13 to 14 hands. *Colour*, grey, black, bay, brown, dun, with occasional roans and chestnuts. *Body*, compact, deep, standing on short legs and covering a lot of ground. Riding *shoulders* (*i.e.* well sloped and not thick and heavy). Well-balanced *head* and *neck*, and a free, easy action and true movement. *Bone*, clean, hard, and flat, measuring 7 to 8 inches below the knee.

The predominant colour is grey, comprising more than half the total number of ponies registered. Blacks are a little more numerous than browns and bays. Dun, the typical and original colour of the Connemara, is now very scarce.

As has been shown, the breed of Connemara Pony is without question an ancient one, and there can be little doubt that the pony as found in Connemara itself is a tough, wiry and altogether typical native pony. Like all such, it thrives on poor keep and, as with other native breeds, seems to do better and retain its type better this way than if stable-fed. It is to be hoped that the true Connemara type will be jealously guarded and retained.

The English Connemara Pony Society now recognise a height limit of 14·2 hands. This recognition curbs the natural tendency of breeders to increase the size, which generally means loss of character. It is indeed essential to retain the true characteristics which are exemplified in the Irish-bred pony.

BREED SOCIETIES : Connemara Pony Breeders' Society and English Connemara Pony Society.

CRIOLLO

The Criollo is a cross between pure-bred horses and original Arab and Barb strains brought to South America through Spain at the time of the Conquest. Having suffered rigorous natural selection covering a period of some three hundred years of wild life, their chief characteristics and qualities of great hardiness and ability to live under exposure have been attained.

At the time of the invasion, the Spanish cavalry ranked as the highest to be found in Europe. In the formation of the Criollo, the oriental blood brought by the Moors to Spain was more potent than that of the horses existing in the Iberian Peninsula, by reason of its greater purity and selection, which lasted through eight centuries of

Mohammedan domination, and in consequence, it may be assumed, had considerable influence on the conquest of the New World.

In the South American pampas, driven into a wild environment following the destruction of Buenos Aires by the Indians, new natural selection began to take place, resulting in much physical perfection due to the severe struggle for existence. The weak and organically unsound perished, while the survivors became the progenitors of the Criollo breed. Such formidable disadvantages as prairie fires, great changes of temperature, dust storms, frosts and floods (not to mention wild dogs) had to be contended with. No doubt it is to the advantage of the horse that he has acquired the peculiarly helpful and characteristic colouring of khaki or dun, which is similar to that of the sandy wastes, straw, or burnt-up pastures or gravel of the countryside. In short, the Criollo adopts protective colouring, as do many other animals and plants in nature.

It is small wonder that the breed is outstanding in those virtues which are so necessary to the real utility horse. The Criollo has figured largely and successfully in many endurance tests, both official and otherwise. It may be noted here that the two famous horses " Mancha " and " Gato " were Criollos, and that they, at the ages of 15 and 16, took part in that epic of endurance when they carried Professor A. F. Tschiffely from Buenos Aires to New York, overcoming incredible difficulties and covering 13,350 miles at an average of 26·5 miles on each day's journey, and achieving a record in altitude of 19,250 feet. An outstanding incident of this amazing journey was that they travelled 93 miles across a desert in Ecuador without water in a temperature of 120 degrees,

Description. Dun, striped or skewbald. Medium-sized. Weight, about 940 lb. Height, 13·3 to 14·3 hands. Head, broad at base, poll narrow, broad forehead with plenty of skull, but narrow face. Neck, of medium size. Withers, muscular and clearly defined. Shoulders, semi-oblique. Generous ribs, showing little light under body. Back, short and deep. Croup, semi-oblique. Forearms and legs, broad and muscular. Cannon-bone short with tendons well separated. Joints clean and rounded. Chestnuts small and only in the region of the hocks. Pasterns medium length. Character and disposition, bright and active.

The illustration shows a very ideal type of animal, short legs, a good shoulder, wonderful middle and quarters, a very good length of rein, and altogether a very pleasant horse to look at. No one who has seen or looked at photographs of " Mancha " and " Gato " would suggest that they have any great resemblance to the animal shown here. They are in fact more true to the real type, which is essentially a very hard-working horse. On the other hand, they claim the clean, hard legs, the strong and fine body and good quarters of the horse illustrated. Having regard to the work which this horse has been called upon to carry out in the past, and is in fact now doing in great numbers in South America, it is not surprising that it has an admirable framework on the best of legs.

BREED SOCIETY : Registered in the Argentine Stud Book.

This pony is a native of the North of England,
and has inhabited its eastern side from time
immemorial. A backbone known as the Pennine
Range runs roughly from north to south and from
the west came the Fell pony, while from the east
came the Dales. Originally, the two were identical
in type and indistinguishable except territorially—
the one was the same as the other except in name.
Now, the Dales is the larger of the two by perhaps
two inches, and it is of more stocky build, the
result of the introduction of cart-horse blood,
mainly Clydesdale or something akin to it.

The Dales Pony was always a weight-carrying
type, and for generations in the last century was
used for carrying lead from the mines in

Northumberland and Durham to the docks in convoys. The ponies were not led, but walked in orderly fashion, controlled by a rider. The weight carried was very great (in all about 16 st.) on either side of the body, and the weekly distance was 240 miles—a notable feat. To this, no doubt, must be attributed their soundness and that they are free and active workers.

To meet the calls of the market, the modern Dales has lost much of its mountain and moorland character, and indeed it is doubtful whether it can be claimed as such. They make, however, a fine type, and a few of the true type do still exist, but they are largely now a cross-bred.

A description of the true Dales pony may be given as follows. They stand up to 14·2 hands and many are jet black, other prevailing colours being bay, brown and occasionally grey, while chestnuts, piebalds and skewbalds are never seen. They are possessed of much fine hair on their heels, which is counted as important. Action is very good, the feet being put down straight and true, though it is not a rare occurrence for some to go wide behind.

The head is neat and pony-like, with small ears neatly set, and with a fine jaw and throat. The neck tends to shortness with shoulders too steep and straight. Back, loins and hind-quarters are all that can be desired, being ample, strong and full, and the ribs are well-sprung. The tail is not set high as in some of the mountain and moorland breeds.

The feet, legs and joints are all very good, and so too are the knees and hocks, and for its size the pony displays great bone. The whole appearance of the pony gives the impression of exceptional strength in relation to its size The breed is very largely free from hereditary unsoundness, and in view of the climatic conditions offered by the country, it is naturally extremely hardy. It is claimed of the pony that it is easily broken and will do all the work required on a small farm. Though of course, subject to market variations, the Dales is a pony which fetches a good price, on account of its extreme utility.

It may be noted here that the working pony for agriculture has never been in great demand in England, certainly not to the same extent as it has been in many parts of Europe, notably in Scandinavian countries. In Scotland, however, there has been a considerable call for such, especially from the crofters on the small farms and holdings in the innumerable islands and on the mainland. With its docility, activity, strength and general hardiness, the Dales Pony is hard to beat for this purpose.

The future of the Dales Pony must to a large extent depend upon the demand or lack of it for the working pony between the shafts. It may be that in many of the larger towns of England and Scotland there will be a demand for such by the small tradesmen, and while that demand lasts the Dales should find a place. It is sufficient to look at the illustration shown here, without even looking closely at the detailed description, to realise that the pony is also admirably built for the smallholder or farmer, but, like all horses and ponies which in the past have found their market as working animals, as distinct from those acquired for pleasure, its future can hardly be said to be assured.

BREED SOCIETY : The Dales Pony Improvement Society.

The indigenous Danish horse was a small, thick-set animal, which later on was crossed with Dutch, Spanish, Turkish and English Thoroughbred blood. Thus were created Danish breeds such as the Frederiksberg, the name of which was taken from the place near Copenhagen, where a great stud existed from 1562 to 1862. There was also the Jutland breed, which was a strong cart-horse very much resembling the Schleswig. The province of Schleswig, which belonged to Denmark, was a great asset in Danish horse-breeding before it was taken over by Prussia. In some coast districts and on certain of the islands there is still seen a sturdy pony much resembling the ponies of Sweden and Finland. To the same group belongs the Iceland Pony, which is very active and hardy.

DARTMOOR

The rugged waste of Dartmoor, in the extreme south-west of England, with its grim and towering tors, its rock-strewn slopes and forbidding bogs— offering at best but the poorest feed, would hardly commend itself to the uninformed as a suitable ground for feeding ponies ; yet here are bred the famous Dartmoor ponies. Here for centuries unknown the Dartmoor has lived and multiplied, while watchful and wise Nature has seen to it that only the fittest survived. Thus it happens that, in common with the other mountain and moorland breeds of the British Isles, a pony, quite indigenous and quite distinctive, roams this bleak countryside in a practically wild state, breeding and literally, when the land is mantled in snow, scratching for an existence These ponies remain entirely unhandled unless rounded-up for sale, and few of the mares and still fewer stallions ever have a hand laid on them except for branding purposes.

Essentially a riding-pony, the Dartmoor, if handled young, makes as good a riding-pony as can be found, and in size and conformation is much akin to its neighbour the Exmoor, both of which breeds can make a long-honoured claim to be good ponies for the young. Nevertheless, in spite of their small size, they are up to a surprising amount of weight ; yet fashion and a misguided prejudice decrees that as soon as a child grows any length of leg, a pony inches higher must be procured. Only within the confines of Dartmoor and Exmoor can these small ponies be seen carrying the adult, with supreme ease and with safety to the rider.

The Dartmoor is a good-looking pony, compact, the best of them conforming well to the accepted standard of any riding-horse or pony, being possessed also of a certain elegance which is very pleasing. It is long-lived, and will see a big family of children through from oldest to youngest and then give good service when passed on to another household. As with all the mountain and moorland breeds of the British Isles, the pure-bred Dartmoor is invaluable as foundation stock, as the records of many of them have shown times without number. Bred up from these excellent foundation ponies, as well as from the Exmoor and Welsh mountain ponies, hunters, hacks and children's ponies have appeared as prizewinners on countless occasions and at the most important shows throughout the length and breadth of the British Isles.

Description. *Height,* not exceeding 12·2 hands. *Colour,* bay, black or brown preferred, but no colours barred except skewbalds and piebalds. *Head,* should be well set on and bloodlike. *Neck,* strong but not too heavy, and neither long nor short. Stallions moderate crest. *Back, loins and hind-quarters,* strong and well covered with muscle. *Ears,* very small and alert. *Feet,* tough and good shaped. *Action,* low, free, typical hack and riding action. *Tail,* set high and full.

For some long while past breeders of the true Dartmoor Pony have suffered a period of great anxiety. Up to perhaps the early days of the present century the habitat of the pony was roamed by the true Dartmoor Pony. To meet the need for very small ponies to work in the mines, certain moormen, without regard to the retention of the pure breed, introduced Shetland stallions indiscriminately to the moors, with the result that the Dartmoor-Shetland cross obtained a very strong footing, and as such cross-breeding was carried out in a very haphazard way many small ponies of most indifferent, and sometimes degenerate, type, multiplied to the exclusion of the true Dartmoor.

The Dartmoor Pony Society, The British Horse Society and others have made strenuous efforts to remove this trouble, but it seems that even the Ministry of Agriculture and Fisheries is powerless in the matter. It is to the credit of the Society and a few individual breeders that they have in small numbers retained the purity of the breed. It is now bred in considerable numbers outside the confines of Dartmoor.

BREED SOCIETY : The Dartmoor Pony Society.

DON

This well-known breed is ranked now as a high-class saddle horse and is found in the districts bordering the Don and Volga rivers. It was originally a small breed, but efforts to increase its size and improve on its conformation were achieved by the introduction during the 19th century and onwards of Persian and Karabakh blood. Whole studs of these Karabakh horses were from time to time purchased in the Caucasus and driven overland to the banks of the Don river for the purposes described. The amazing powers of endurance of the Don horses are almost unbelievable. It was with these incredibly tough horses that the Cossacks harassed Napoleon's ill-fated army in 1812, marching not only on Paris but afterwards back across Europe into Russia again, a feat unequalled in cavalry history. The Cossacks, who originally guarded the Russian frontiers from nomadic Tartar invaders, maintain their horses in the traditional droves which still roam the plains to-day.

Many Don horses are of the much-admired golden colour inherited from the Karabakh breed. A number of different types are discernible, but together with the golden coat colour, the most sought-after are those showing Persian characteristics—noble expressions, fine heads, and elegance of conformation : in short, they are looked upon as the Russian saddle-horses of perfection.

DUTCH DRAUGHT

The Dutch Draught Horse belongs to the most massively built and most heavily muscled breeds of Europe. The official descent can be traced back to the second half of the last century by means of the Stud Books of the Royal Netherlands Draught Horse Society, which covers the whole of the country and includes all Dutch Draught Horse breeders, its aim being the improvement and promotion of Draught Horses in the Netherlands.

In order to consolidate the characteristics of the breed, no horses of unknown pedigree have since 1925 been entered in its Stud Book, and this is the only one in Holland that is based upon absolutely pure breeding, since only the progeny of officially registered parents is made eligible for entry. Horses are not entered until their pedigree has been carefully checked and an accurate description has been supplied. When a registered horse is over two and a half years, it can be entered in the Preferential Stud Book, after passing a special examination of its conformation. For an even further grading of Preferential mares and stallions, inter-provincial prize examinations are held at regular intervals, and once a year a National Show is held, at which not only conformation but also breeding achievements and pedigree are judged.

Draught Horse breeding in the Netherlands has developed rapidly and has been pursued in all provinces for many decades, and is now very successfully carried on throughout the country, on all types of soil, including sandy, peaty and heavy silty soils. Today the breed is recognised as being docile under all circumstances, willing, active, with a pleasant, courageous disposition. It is famous for its exceptionally long working life—it can be used for light work on the farm at two years or even under—for its durability, great fecundity and excellent breeding performance. It has a quiet and intelligent temperament and great stamina. Last, but not least, it is very moderate in its feeding requirements and can be successfully maintained on plain fare.

Description. The Dutch Draught Horse is a massive, hard, deep animal of heavy build. The neck is very short, carrying a not too heavy head, with withers little developed and shoulders more often than not heavily loaded. The legs are well-placed, correctly shaped and heavily muscled, with good feet ; the fore-quarters are well developed and massive, the back strong and wide with well-sprung ribs, and the hind-quarters wide, heavy and powerful. The tail is low-set, the croup sloping more perhaps than in any other breed. *Colour*, bay, chestnut or grey : black rarely seen.

The Exmoor pony is the descendant of the native British wild horse and is believed to be an indigenous animal that has been preserved in its aboriginal state from the earliest times to the present day. This apparently is borne out by the research work which has been done and is to some extent being continued in the department of anatomy in the Royal (Dick) Veterinary College, Edinburgh.

The large tract of wild country known as Exmoor lies in the south-west of England and is contained in the extreme west of the county of Somerset, though some adjacent moors lie in the county of Devon. It is a wild part for England, sparsely inhabited, and the ponies run wild over a series of high, bleak moorlands. Although the " keep " is of a better quality than that to be found in the New Forest, they have a hard life in

95

winter and they can claim, because of this and the survival of the fittest, to rank with the other mountain and moorland breeds for stamina and naturally acquire that characteristic sure-footedness common to these groups of native ponies.

An excellent child's pony, the true and pure native Exmoor owes much to the Acland family, which has consistently maintained the old type of pony. As with all other of England's native pony breeds, its origin is obscure and of great antiquity. Historians seem to agree, however, that it is strictly indigenous and is probably as old as the first inhabitant.

Experiments have been made from time to time, as with the other native breeds, to increase the size of the pony by the introduction of alien blood, but the attempts met with varying success. Lovely ponies have been bred, but these, it has been found, do not stand up to the rigours of the wild winter storms.

The true-bred pony roaming the moors remains small, hardy and true to type. Let anyone see these mealy-nosed ponies, living on grass, probably never having tasted corn in their lives, carrying full-grown men through a long day with the Devon and Somerset Hounds up to the finish. Let him ponder for a moment on the animals' strength, courage, speed and endurance, and he will not be surprised that the merit of the breed has been discovered and appreciated.

Large numbers of these ponies have been seen in England, not only in harness but more particularly as children's riding-ponies. They are rather wild in coming to hand, but if taken off the moor young enough and handled with care and consideration, they make good and lovable mounts for young people, and give honest service through a long life. Their outstanding characteristic is that they all have a mealy nose or muzzle and show no white markings whatsoever. When seen at the National Pony Society's Annual Breed Show in London, the Exmoor has compared favourably with the other breeds of mountain and moorland ponies, and has done well in the classes under saddle. Many a young one bought in the rough at the annual sale at Bampton, in Devon, has taught several in a family to ride and has been received by other families with satisfaction for the same purpose.

Description. *Head,* rather long with deep-set jaw and broad forehead. Ears short and thick with mealy colour inside. Eyes, large, wide apart and prominent (locally called the " Toad eye "). *Body,* chest, deep and wide. Back, medium length and strong with powerful loins. Shoulders, set well back, making the Exmoor pony very sure footed. *Legs,* clean and short, with neat, hard feet. *Coat,* texture different from that of any other native breed. It is springy and harsh and in winter there is seldom any bloom on it, but in summer the coat is close and hard and shines like brass. *Colour,* brown, bay or dun. No white markings *anywhere.* *Height,* when full grown the maximum is 12·2 hands for a mare and 12·3 hands for a stallion.

BREED SOCIETY : The Exmoor Pony Society.

Upwards of sixty years ago the Fell Pony was used to carry the lead from the mines to the docks on Tyneside, in Northern England. Loose-headed and in droves of twenty, these ponies carried 16 st. of lead, pannier fashion, 8 st. a side. In charge of a mounted man this drove was kept together at a steady walk, and 240 miles per week was the pony's job. These were the Dales and Fell ponies. In those days there was no distinction between the breeds.

The Pennine Range of hills is the backbone running down the North of England separating Westmorland and Cumberland from Northumberland, Durham and Yorkshire. It is a great range of wild moorland, with but few scattered farms, where only the hardiest animals can stand the climate Roughly, from the crown of the hills away to the west and in the mountains of Westmorland and Cumberland, overshadowing Windermere, Ullswater, Derwentwater and the lesser lakes, the Fell ponies are to be found running wild, and finding what they can to sustain life on these precipitous and none-too-hospitable hills. On the other side, away to the east, is the home of the Dales pony—his brother breed—a rather more stocky pony and standing an inch or two higher.

Although formerly used as a pack pony, carrying great weight, the Fell pony is an excellent riding-pony; indeed, as a general utility ride-and-drive, he is hard to beat. An average height is about 13·2 hands. From the admirable show type seen at the National Pony Society's Annual Show sometimes held in Roehampton, London, to the rough and rather uncouth animal seen in his native surroundings, the Fell seems to breed wonderfully true to type; indeed, of all the mountain and moorland breeds of Britain, none breeds more truly to type than the Fell.

Description. The colours are black, dark brown, dark bay and sometimes grey or dun. Perhaps the colour most frequently found is black with no white markings, and this is mostly favoured. In appearance the pony is of the true mountain type, powerfully built and alert-looking. The hair both on mane and tail is very long and distinctly curly, while the heels are abundantly covered in " feather." The legs are set squarely, with well-developed and prominent knees, while the hocks are wide, large and clean, standing parallel with the body and well let-down with bone below the knee, measuring sometimes 8½ to 9¼ inches below the hock. Girth measurement should be about 6 ft. The foot should be round, open and of good shape, with dense and unblemished horn. The shoulders are long, sloping and well-laid back, and fine at the points, with a good neck of reasonable length and a defined crest. The Fell must have a pony head with sharp, well-placed ears, and it may be noted that lop ears are unknown in the breed. The body is very strong and muscular with well-sprung ribs, the quarters generous, with tail set fairly high and carried gaily.

Reference has been made to the alliance of the Fell with the Dales Pony, and although there is now some difference in height and a very considerable difference in appearance (as will be seen from the illustrations under both breeds) the fact remains that they were at one time practically identical, the difference in name being purely territorial. A great change, however, now separates the two, and this has been brought about by cross-breeding, and by the introduction of heavy horse blood. The Fell Pony Society and the pony's breeders are very jealous of the purity of the breed and are unlikely to permit the introduction of any alien blood so far as can be seen. Of all our mountain and moorland breeds there are few more easily recognised than the black or brown Fell Pony, with its very long and rather ample and well-curled mane and tail and, for a pony, generously feathered heels.

BREED SOCIETY : The Fell Pony Society.

Norway has two very well-known breeds of horses, the Fjord and the Gudbrandsdal. The former, the Vestland horse, though stockily built shows quite an amount of quality, due no doubt to the fact that it is well saturated with Arab blood. The colour is usually grey.

Mention should also be made of a horse of the Baltic States which is derived from the original small Esthonian or Smudish (Zmudzin) native horse. This belongs to the same group of North European horses as the Scandinavian and other native breeds. In Lithuania the native horse was crossed with an East Prussian breed, giving in result the Prussian Lithuanian. The most successful, however, was the cross of a native horse with a heavier horse, giving a thick, sturdy horse.

FRIESIAN

This breed is entirely indigenous to the Netherlands, and as it is found today its production is limited in the main to the province of Friesland, where it is claimed that it is bred with increasing success in the so-called meadow districts and in sandy soil areas. Its popularity is said to be largely based on the admirable character of the horse, for it excels in docility, willingness and cheerful temperament, enabling unskilled labourers to handle the horse without risk. It is, furthermore, an economical feeder and will keep its condition on rations which would mean starvation to some breeds.

A finely chiselled head with small ears is carried on a shapely neck with an exceptionally long mane, which has been known to reach the ground. The back is strong, and ribs deep and well-rounded, though the tail, which carries much hair, is set rather low. The legs also are heavily covered with hair, sometimes right up to the knee joint, and it should be noted that the colour is always black, though a small star is occasionally met with. Neither docking nor trimming of the mane or tail is tolerated in the Friesian horse, and would bar registration in the Friesian Stud Book, which was founded in 1879.

Prior to being entered in the Stud Book, the stallions and mares have to comply with high standards of conformation and pedigree, purity of breed being of major importance. After a special examination they are submitted to a strict veterinary inspection.

During the years of the Second World War breeding activities greatly increased, since in this period all sorts of difficulties were put in the way of mechanised traction. The efficient management of the Stud Books and the excellent breeding material available made it possible to create a large horse population of a quality even better than before. Because of its impressive colour, its tractability and natural balanced carriage, the Friesian stallion has of late become popular as a circus horse, and it is claimed that the demand is ever increasing. As a nation the Dutch have always been very attracted to the harness horse in the show ring, and it is a frequent and popular spectacle to see in the ring Friesian horses drawing Friesian gigs, the occupants being, perhaps, a gentleman with his lady, both in the old Friesian costume, while to complete the picture the Friesian National Anthem is played.

GELDERLAND

Horses of this breed, which derives its name from the Dutch province of Gelderland, where breeding is still carried on quite extensively, originate from a very old native breed which was crossed many years ago with such stallions as English Thoroughbreds, Holsteins and Anglo-Normans. During the past few decades, the main consideration has been consolidation of type, with very remarkable results, for the breed has greatly improved of recent years, the modern horse being wide and deep, yet of beautiful build, with a very stylish action. A docile farm horse and an excellent saddle-horse, it is claimed to be an unsurpassable show horse in Holland. In the past several Royal Studs, including Great Britain's, have been regular buyers of these horses. Height ranges from 15·2 to 16 hands, although larger animals are occasionally met with.

GIDRAN and NONIUS

A Hungarian breed, the Gidran, larger than the Shagya, was formed by crossing native mares with English Thoroughbred and English half-bred stallions. The Gidran is a big saddle-horse, standing about 16 hands, with a beautiful characteristic head and good conformation, and is usually chestnut or brown in colour. It has a great capacity for galloping and is a comfortable and good-looking cavalry horse. Its breeding is very popular not only in Hungary but also in other countries. In Poland in particular, Prince Sanguszko's stud at Gumniska produced a very useful horse, deep in body with typical conformation.

Better known, perhaps, than the Gidran, is the Hungarian breed Nonius, which owes its name to the Anglo-Norman stallion of that name. This horse was used as a sire with great success and is considered as the founder of the breed. There are two well-recognised types of this breed : the Large Nonius and the Small Nonius. The first type is a rather massive, big-boned animal, standing very often 17 hands, while the Small Nonius is much lighter in type and general appearance and stands about 15·2 hands. Both these varieties, however, are not genetically bred as such, but they come out in breeding ; one may, indeed, have Large and Small Nonius sometimes from the same mare. The Nonius has a very quiet disposition, excellent action, and makes a very good horse for both agricultural and military purposes ; the Large Nonius makes a good horse-artillery wheeler. It is recognised as a drawback to this breed that they are not hard enough. Their usual colour is dark bay.

GRONINGEN

Essentially a Dutch farm horse, the Groningen can be used successfully as a heavy-weight saddle-horse and is also an excellent carriage horse, showing speedy, responsive and stylish action, with much natural bearing and great endurance. Of good conformation, this horse has a strong back and deep body, with legs and feet of excellent substance, and a very refined head and neck, yet thrives on poorish fare. His strongest characteristics are said to be docility and obedience. Height ranges from 15·2 to 16 hands, although larger specimens are permitted. Despite a comparatively heavy weight, the horse is primarily a light draught horse, of pure breed and good pedigree.

Very much resembling the Swedish and Finnish native pony, being also hardy, strong and rather small, are two Norwegian breeds. Most of the horses are to be found on the north or west coasts of Norway, and are usually dun with a black stripe along the back. The Gudbrandsdal Valley (Ostland) breed is very well known abroad and in Sweden and Poland, and can be seen all over Norway. It is a horse of medium size with a good gait.

Any consideration of this horse should be made in connection with all the Scandinavian and North European horses which, as remarked elsewhere, are remarkably similar in many characteristics.

The name " hack " is essentially British and is
of quite ancient origin, but it must not be confused
with the word " hackney," for in modern times
the latter indicates the harness-horse, while the
hack denotes the refined riding-horse. Furthermore it should be noted that the hack is in no
sense an established breed, but as it is most
definitely a type it has its place in this book.

The hack in Britain is any horse or pony which
is suitable for riding, but for the purposes of this
short note it is desirable to treat it according to
the standards laid down by the British Hack and
Cob Society, which decrees that it must not
exceed in height 15·3 hands, and not being an
established breed it can be of any colour.

To win in the show-rings of Great Britain, Eire or Northern Ireland, any horse conforming to the height and having the necessary quality and manners may be of any breed or any admixture of breeds, but in practice, as extreme refinement and performance are the principal factors, it follows that the winner is usually found in the Thoroughbred. All, therefore, that is expected in the Thoroughbred of great quality (and it should be noted many Thoroughbreds fail considerably in this respect) are needed in the winning hack. Indeed, those points, such as the refined head to fit the neck of true proportions, the well-laid-back shoulder, the pronounced, though not exaggerated wither, short back with big girth and well-sprung ribs and powerful quarters, must be found, if anything, in exaggerated proportions in the winning hack. It is obvious, too, that the legs must be clean and strong, and in his movements he must be absolutely true and level.

It must also be emphasised that the winning hack must be, if possible, entirely without blemish ; with perfection of form must go perfection of manners, which must be impeccable in all respects. He must stand immobile while the acts of mounting and dismounting are performed ; he must walk with ease and freedom and use his shoulders, turning his head neither to right nor left. At the trot, as with the walk, he should be capable of collection or extension as asked ; and the same applies to the canter, in which he must show no sign of knee or harness action. Furthermore, he must be able to perform such movements of change of leg, passage and reining back as the judge may call upon him to perform.

It should be borne in mind when picturing and assessing a high-class hack that he must give the impression of being under complete control, willing to answer the aids applied by his rider with a minimum of effort by each. He must give the appearance not only of extreme balance and beauty of action, but of controlled and elegant airiness, the beautiful horse in appearance, moving with action so refined that he gives to his rider everything which the accomplished horseman could possibly wish.

Although it has been mentioned before that the show winning hack is usually a Thoroughbred, it may be that, although it has prevailed for a number of years, this is something which will pass, giving way, perhaps, to the most refined type of Anglo-Arab or part-bred Arab. If such a state of affairs comes about, it may be that as much as anything it will be on account of the intelligence, manners and more tractable characteristics of the Arab. Already in some of the highest-class Thoroughbred company evidence of this has been forthcoming, and certainly in the show pony, which is analogous to this, the Anglo-Arab and part-bred Arab have now obtained a very strong hold, and it is conceivable that what the show pony world finds today, the hack world will discover tomorrow.

Leaving aside the question of a desirable breed or cross for the ideal hack, the true test must always be found in the horse that can produce in superlative company, beauty, grace, refinement of action, impeccable manners and an overriding aura of charm. For that indeed is the picture of the show hack. For the workaday hack that cannot hope to excel in the show ring, it can only be said that the nearer it attains to this pattern of excellence, the greater will be its worth as a hack.

BREED SOCIETY : The British Show Hack and Cob Association.

The modern Hackney is a harness-horse with a characteristic high-stepping, long, round striding trotting action, which can most truly be described as brilliant.

The immediate ancestor of the modern Hackney is the Norfolk trotter, which sprang from the blood of two horses, an Arab stallion and a Yorkshire stallion, in about 1729. The Norfolk Roadster, as it came to be known, was a powerful, heavily built animal bred for utility, used by farmers and others in their daily work. It possessed both speed and stamina, and had to be up to weight, being often called upon to carry not only the farmer to market but his wife as well, riding pillion behind him. The most famous of that breed was the " Norfolk Cob," bred from Burgess's " Fireaway " in the early 1820s. He is said to have trotted 24 miles in the hour, and is definitely recorded as having done 2 miles in 5 minutes 4 seconds. Another famous trotter, " Nonpareil," was driven 100 miles in 9 hours 56 minutes 57 seconds.

As is obvious from its description, the Hackney has Arab blood in its veins, and almost every Hackney sire can trace its descent directly back to the Darley Arabian, through his son " Flying Childers." Another famous sire was " Sampson," whose grandson, " Messenger," was the foundation of the present American trotting horse. During the 19th century, with the advent of the railway, the Norfolk breed fell into disuse, to be revived again by the Hackney Horse Society in the animal that we know today.

The ultimate origins of the Hackney, however, go back far into English history, the trotting horse, as distinguished from the ambler and the galloper, being recognised in very early times, being definitely mentioned as such in 1303. There was also at one time a strong infusion of Spanish Andalusian blood. The name itself is derived from the Norman French word *haquenée.*

Chief characteristics, in addition to brilliant and fiery paces, are : small, convex head, small muzzle ; large eyes and small ears ; longish, thick-set neck ; powerful shoulders and low withers ; compact body without great depth of chest ; tail set and carried high, usually docked ; short legs and strong hocks well let down ; well-shaped feet ; fine silky coat. Most usual colours, dark brown, black, bay and chestnut. Height varies from 14·3 to 15·3 hands, sometimes reaching 16·2.

Both in motion and at rest it has highly distinctive and readily observable characteristics. Shoulder action is free, with a high, ground-covering knee action, the foreleg being thrown well forward, not just up and down, with that slight pause of the foot at each stride which gives it its peculiar grace of movement, appearing to fly over the ground. Action of the hind legs is the same to a lesser degree. In a good Hackney the action must be straight and true, with no dishing or throwing of the hoofs from side to side. At rest the Hackney stands firm and foursquare, forelegs straight, hind legs well back, so that it covers the maximum ground; the head is held high, ears pricked, with a general impression of alertness and of being on springs.

In these days of mechanised transport it would not be surprising if it had to be recorded that the Hackney Horse, which exists today purely as a pleasure horse, was declining to complete extinction at a rapid pace. Quite the reverse, however, can be recorded, the credit for which lies with the horse itself (and with the horse is included the Hackney Pony), with all its spectacular and dynamic action and the large and increasing number of breeders and admirers of the Hackney. During the period between the wars, a steady improvement was noticed in the Hackney, and since the Second World War this has become even more pronounced, so that today it is no great exaggeration to say that the unbeatable, be it horse or pony, has become beatable.

This is a state of affairs which must give great satisfaction to all who follow the fortunes of the Hackney, which, by the way, is recognised as being, with the show jumper, the most popular entrant in the show ring, each in its own way providing a maximum of violent but controlled activity. It should be mentioned that this last general commentary upon this breed applies equally to the Hackney Pony, and although its evolution differs to some extent from that of the horse, it is a replica on a smaller scale.

BREED SOCIETY : The Hackney Horse Society.

HACKNEY PONY

The evolution of the Hackney Pony is some-what obscure as to date, though it is in fact a smaller edition of the Hackney Horse, which is of some antiquity. It is generally believed that the pony's first appearance was through a 14-hand Hackney Pony stallion foaled in the North of England in 1866 and registered as " Sir George," and sired by a horse which was of the purest Yorkshire blood named " Sportsman," although nothing is known of the breeding of the dam. From such breeding, however, came perhaps the most spectacular exhibit to be seen in English horse shows today.

Owing to the decline of the use of the harness-horse and pony, which has been progressive in England for many years, the Hackney is seen almost exclusively in the show-ring, where he is most popular. There the demand is for the most extravagant action which it is possible to produce in a horse, and nothing short of this can carry the animal to any degree of success. The action must be spectacular, fluid and extravagant, with knees raised to the extremity and feet flung forward with rounded action, avoiding any heaviness of fore-hand or going into the ground. The hocks must be brought right under the body and raised almost to touch it. The whole effect must be arresting and startling, showing extreme brilliance. The best of these ponies fetch high prices both for the home and export trade.

The Hackney Pony must be of true pony type, especially as to the head, and the small horse, as distinct from the pony, must be avoided. Of late years, in spite of the development of more extravagant action, there is a tendency in the breed to lose a certain straightness of action, many otherwise good ponies going too close in front with hocks away.

Ponies whose action is not sufficiently extravagant for the show-ring find a not-too-ready market. To the extent that they can be absorbed into the harness market, they serve a very good purpose, for they are possessed of hard legs and will stand up to wear in spite of popular belief to the contrary. That they are active workers may be assumed. Owing to the enormous amount of muscular development in the hocks, the Hackney Pony is much in demand as a show jumper, at which sport it excels. Up to the early years of the present century the pony was much used by tradesmen for delivery purposes, owing to its flash appearance and the fact that it is an active and honest worker. In addition, it was looked upon as a good advertisement for any tradesman.

Description. Pony character throughout. A long neck, good shoulders and a compact, strong body with hard limbs and well-defined tendons. Colours are mostly bays, browns and blacks.

BREED SOCIETY : The Hackney Horse Society.

HAFFLINGER

The Hafflinger Pony is a Tyrolese breed and represents a small but very thick mountain horse, with plenty of bone and heavy head, which he usually carries close to the ground while climbing. Owing to his great qualities of strength, sure-footedness and quite good movement, he makes an excellent pack and draught horse, used to a great extent in the agriculture and forestry industries in the mountains. Just before the Second World War he attracted a great amount of attention from the German authorities, who gave much support to his breeding. The Hafflinger stallions were reared in the Central Stud at Piber (Austria). The average height of the pony is just under 14 hands, having a rather long body, and being usually dark bay or black in colour.

The Hanoverian breed, as it is known today, is a comparatively modern production, owing its origin to the influence of our own Hanoverian kings, who, from the time of George I down to 1837, took a great interest in the horse of their native Hanover and sent many English Thorough-breds to cross with the existing German breeds.

These breeds were sprung from the German Great Horse of the Middle Ages, which was a descendant of the animals that carried the Frankish horsemen when, under Charles Martel, they met and defeated the Saracens at the Battle of Poitiers in 732, one of the decisive battles of the world. The descent of these animals may be traced from the Eastern and Southern European breeds of pre-Christian times, mixed with the horses of a German tribe, the Tencteri, who settled on the left bank of the Rhine about A.D. 100 and who " were distinguished from all other German tribes by their love of horses and their finely organised cavalry."

From the time of the Franks, the German horse developed and became the great war horse of European armoured chivalry, and Blunderville's description of him is worth recording :

The Almaine is commonlie a great horse, and though not finelie, yet verie stronglie made, and therefore more meete for the shocke than to pass a cariere, or to make a swift manage, because they are very grosse and heavie. . . . The desposition of this Horse (his heavy mould considered) is not evill, for he is verie tractable, and will labour indiffirentlie by the way, but his pace for the most part is a verie hard trot.

The horses of Flanders, Cleves and so on were all varieties of the same type.

With the advent of gunpowder and the disappearance of armour the type had to be modified again, and German breeders developed the 17th and 18th century light and heavy cavalry horse, falling into three main groups—Hanoverian, Mecklenburg and Danish.

This old Hanoverian breed was then, as we have seen, interbred with the English horses sent over by the Hanoverian Georges, and had finally disappeared by about the middle of the 18th century, to be replaced by the modern Hanoverian, a close and direct descendant of the famous fathers of the English Thoroughbred, the Darley and Godolphin Arabians and the Byerley Turk.

The object of the breeders was to produce strong half-breds of good quality, the lighter type of which are used for riding and the heavy type for harness. They were bred principally on the pastures in the valleys of the Elbe, Weser and Ems Rivers, the chief studs being at Celle and Osnabrück.

There developed a number of distinct families, named after early sires : Adeptus, Flick, Schlutter, Kingdown XX, Nelusko, Spot, Jason, Hogarth. The most famous and predominant are the Adeptus line, descended from the Darley Arabian, and the Flick line, which carries the blood of the Godolphin Arabian. Nearly 60 per cent. of all Hanoverian horses bred up to 1914 were of one or other of these two strains.

A study of the picture of " Adeptus XX " (1880–1904), a fine specimen of the breed, shows a handsome animal, heavily built but with plenty of " blood " about it, powerful quarters and shoulders, thick neck, intelligent head and good clean legs.

There are few breeds of horses on the Continent better known than the Hanoverian and, as is shown, it has from time to time been intermixed with the Thoroughbred and the three famous Arabians. At different times many Hanoverians, or close crosses to them, were seen in England, and there is no doubt not only that they represented a fine and impressive type of horse, but also had much real equine worth. In considering this breed and its history, the student is advised to do so in connection with that of the Holstein, which it somewhat resembles.

HIGHLAND

The largest and strongest of the mountain and moorland group of breeds of Great Britain, the Highland pony is to be found in the highlands of Scotland and certain adjacent islands. The Highland is of great antiquity. It is said that after the Ice Age in Europe there was a movement of ponies towards the west from Northern Asia, the larger ones keeping to the north, now represented by the Scandinavian and Highland ponies, and the smaller going to the south, becoming known by the general term of Eastern Breeds.

Today the Highland pony may be divided into three types : the smaller ponies of Barra and the outer islands standing from 12·2 to 13·2 hands ; the second class is the well-known riding-pony of some 13·2 to 14·2 hands ; the largest and strongest are known as " Mainland " ponies, and stand about 14·2 hands. Highland ponies have had an infusion of alien blood, mostly Arabian.

As a worker the Highlander is immensely strong and very docile. He has always been used to carrying stalkers in the Highlands, and has always been a great stand-by for the crofters in those parts. The pony is first-class for hill work on account of its sure-footedness, and is a well-balanced walker. It is pleasant to ride at its natural paces which are walking and trotting, but many tend to be on the " forehand. "

Description. *Head*, well carried, attractive and broad between prominent, bright eyes ; short between eyes and muzzle, with wide nostrils. Ears short and well set. In profile the breadth rather than the length of the head and jawbone should be pronounced. *Neck*, strong and not short, crest arched, with flowing mane ; throat clean, not too fleshy. *Shoulders*, well set back ; withers not too pronounced. *Body*, back short, with slight natural curve ; chest deep ; ribs deep, well sprung, carried well back. *Quarters* and loins powerful, thighs short and strong. *Tail*, strong and well set on, carried gaily, with a plentiful covering of hair almost to the ground. *Legs*, flat in the bone, flinty to the touch, with a slight fringe of straight silken feather ending in a prominent tuft at the fetlock joint. Forelegs placed well under the weight of the body ; fore-arm strong and knee broad. Oblique pasterns, not too short ; and broad, firm, horny hoofs. *Hocks*, broad, clean, flat and closely set. *Action*, free and straight. *Colour*, black, brown, fox colour with silver mane and tail ; varying dun or grey with no white markings. The eel stripe along back is typical, but not always present.

BREED SOCIETY : The Highland Pony Society.

HOLSTEIN

Another very good German breed, suitable for both riding and driving, is the Holstein Horse, whose Andalusian origin (and oriental according to some believers) is supposed to date back to the 13th century. The horse was bred on very good pastures of alluvial origin on the right bank of the River Elbe, which were very suitable for providing a powerful animal, and in the 16th to 18th centuries this breed was in high esteem not only at home but also abroad, particularly for export to France. The breed fetched good prices and was exported in large numbers, but afterwards it deteriorated.

According to E. Iverson's " Abstracts of Animal Breeding," March 1939, p. 6, " Das Holsteiner Pferd, 1937 " :

from 1825 onwards a reorientation of breeding took place, particularly owing to the introduction of the Yorkshire Coach Horse. The resulting compact conformation combined with a satisfactory gait proved successful, and an increased demand for Holstein horses again caused a serious dearth of breeding of uniform quality. This led to the organisation of breeders and of the central stud at Traventhal. Contrary to the usual policy in German "warm-blood" breeding, the English Thoroughbred influence in Holstein is negligible, but half-bred stallions contributed to the present excellence of the blood.

Usually of brown colouring, the Holstein horse is a very fine, strong animal, with good legs, free action, endurance and gait, and his conformation is different from that of other German "warm-blood" horses. Although of slow growth he enjoys now a very good reputation as a light-draught horse, hunter and even chaser. Just before the Second World War there was a great demand for the Holstein in South America and other countries, while in Germany they were mostly used as artillery horses.

As with the Hanoverian, the Holstein was always a popular horse and one that was found in great numbers, but like all ride-and-drive horses the breed has suffered more seriously than the true riding-horse as the result of mechanisation. As has been pointed out, it has a resemblance to the Hanoverian, and is seen at times as a very handsome horse, although others have not attained a very high standard of looks.

HUNGARIAN SHAGYA

As equine skulls dating from the period of the Magyar invasion show, the Hungarian horse had prevailing characteristics of the wild tarpan (*Equus caballus gmellini*) with certain admixture of the blood of the Mongolian horse (*Equus przevalskii*). It was a hardy, primitive breed, late maturing, small, and possessed of great endurance. Later on numerous Turkish invasions were responsible for introducing to the Hungarian horse a strong dose of oriental blood by crossing with Arab, Turkish and Persian stallions. The Hungarian farmers' horse is a descendant of this horse, although some changes would occur in it because of the large number of half-bred horses which spread their influence all over the country.

It is a light horse standing roughly about 15 hands, with very good strong legs and intelligent head, lively temperament, used for both saddle and harness. It is bred in a rather rough manner, fed only on maize, oat straw and grass, and taken into work as a two-year-old. This native stock was excellent material for establishing the new, popular Hungarian breeds, which were bred on a large scale for military purposes in the days of the Austro-Hungarian Empire.

The best Hungarian breed, which can in fact be considered as a special kind of Arab half-bred, is the Shagya. The name is derived from a stallion of that name which was responsible for the foundation of the breed. There is a tradition still adhered to that stallions of this breed have the same name with the addition of a Roman number, which shows to which generation after the original Shagya the horse belongs. Genetically this breed was very well established, thanks to much careful inbreeding. The Shagya is an extremely hardy horse, standing from 14 to 15 hands, an excellent mover, thriving on very little food and having not only looks but also most of the qualities of Arab. In colour most of them are grey. The horse, being the best light-cavalry and light-carriage horse, is bred all over Hungary and in the neighbouring countries. The main stud is in Babolna. Many of the Shagya stallions after 1918 were imported to Poland and caused great improvement to appear in Polish horse-breeding, especially in the southern part of Poland.

It is not necessary to point out perhaps that horses have been used for the chase for very many centuries, for they have always offered the obvious and the most convenient medium to man seeking and pursuing his quarry, whether boar, stag, fox or hare. The type of animal ridden is now—and always has been—dependent upon the animal hunted, the size and weight of the rider, and the nature of the country hunted. It is clear that the hunter, strictly speaking, is of no particular breed.

If, however, the hunter is considered for hunting at its best in England, Eire, or the United States of America, then the Thoroughbred horse is the one which is considered essential for a country, especially where fences are big and hounds hunt in the main over grass, such as is typified by the shires of England. Apart from this, hunting countries which ride " heavy," that is, where the going may be expected to be deep and holding, obviously require a short-legged and powerful animal ; and to generalise still further, a hilly country requires not only a horse with exceptional shoulders, but one that has natural balance, if its rider is to hunt with safety as well as comfort. In a confined and trappy country where there is much woodland and the fences are very varied in character, a handy horse of reasonable height is indicated ; and it should be emphasised that one of the most important requirements of a hunter in any of the countries suggested, or indeed in any country, good, bad or indifferent, is a horse with plenty of natural intelligence, for a day with hounds can hardly be enjoyed anywhere, at any time, without both horse and rider finding themselves in some sort of difficulty, where it is almost invariably the horse which must save the situation by instant application of its sense of self-preservation.

The show hunter of today, according to British standards, is grouped into three classes—lightweight, 13 st. and under ; middle-weight, over 13 st. and not exceeding 14 st. 7 lb. ; and the heavy-weight hunter, over 14 st. 7 lb. Perhaps the most admired—and certainly the most expensive—hunter, whether a show horse or not, is a Thoroughbred horse up to as much weight as possible, and the more weight he can carry the greater is his market value.

In judging a hunter, a few essentials of vital importance must always be borne in mind. He must, of course, be absolutely sound and stand on the best of legs ; his body must be generous and sufficiently ample to allow heart, lungs and so on to perform their duties under conditions of great exertion ; and, further, he should give his rider as long a rein as possible. His head must be of the right size and his neck obviously of the correct length to assist with the many acts of balancing which he must perform during a hunt. Almost of more importance, if it is possible, the high-class hunter must be courageous and bold, tireless and, as it is said, always able to find an " extra leg " if in trouble. He must not chance his fences, but must stand back and boldly attack each one as he meets it ; such being the case, it is obvious that if the right temperament is there the ideal horse to hunt is the Thoroughbred, or as near as may be to one that is Thoroughbred.

The value of a hunter must in the main be dependent on his ability to perform in a way required of a good hunter following hounds. This, however, does not apply to the show hunter in England, for no certificate or evidence of any kind is required of his performance in that direction, nor is he required to jump obstacles in the show-ring, although now from time to time at some shows this may be a condition of entry.

Under these circumstances, the judging must be based on conformation and, to some extent, type, and largely on action. Furthermore, the judge will ride the exhibit to discover how he would probably behave in the heat of the chase and whether he would be in good control at his fences. How well or ill he can actually perform is a matter for decision by the judge.

BREED SOCIETY : The Hunters' Improvement and National Light Horse Breeding Society.

The ponies of Iceland are not indigenous, but immigrants, and their history is almost exactly contemporaneous with that of the inhabitants. The original settlers in Iceland were two Norwegian *jarls*, Ingolf and Leif, who, refusing to submit to Harold Fairhair when he made himself sole king of all Norway in the year 870, removed themselves to Iceland in 871 and finally settled there in 874. Other settlers followed from Norway, and later in the same century from the Western Isles.

These settlers brought with them their families, household goods and domestic livestock, including ponies. So there is good evidence that the horse was introduced into Iceland from both east and south-west—Norway and Ireland—and the present animal is a mixture of two early varieties of the Celtic type of horse which we find so widely distributed over north and west Europe. (See also Connemara, Norwegian, Shetland, Highland, Scandinavian, etc.) The ultimate place of origin of the south-western or Hebridean stock was Ireland, for there was a good deal of traffic between Ireland and the Hebrides and Iceland. Horses figure also in the Icelandic sagas, two famous ones being Starkad's chestnut stallion and Gunnar's brown described in the " Saga of Burnt Njal."

The Norse settlers in Iceland, in addition to the ordinary domestic uses of their ponies, indulged in the pastime of horse-fighting. The same source tells that " Starkad had a good horse of chestnut hue and it was thought that no horse was his match in fight." And the development of the tragedy depends on the fight between that horse and Gunnar's brown and its sequel. They also ate horse-flesh on special occasions until their conversion to Christianity at the end of the 10th century.

Iceland ponies are usually graded into riding and pack and (to a less extent) draught, although the latter are all rideable if necessary. The riding ponies are broken to an ambling gait. They have been for the thousand or so years of their history the only means of transport in Iceland.

In appearance they are short and stocky, with large heads and intelligent eyes, very short, thick necks, and heavy mane and forelock, and are from 12 to 13 hands. They are hardy in the extreme and possess very keen sight. They also have a pronounced homing instinct, and the customary way of returning a pony after a long trek is to turn it loose, and it will usually find its way home within 24 hours. Little ordinary horse training or horsemastership is possible with them, and the usual method of control is by voice. In character they are docile and friendly, although, like all these small pony breeds, they are sturdily independent by nature.

Attempts to produce a finer, more breedy type of Thoroughbred cross in order to produce a good child's pony have failed, the best characteristic of both strains being lost. It would seem that the Iceland pony is a mixture rather than a breed and will not breed true outside its own blood.

Mention should be made here of a similar type, the ponies of the Faroe Islands. Very much the same in appearance and character, their prevailing colours are dark brown and chestnut and occasionally black, while the most frequent colours of the Iceland pony are grey and dun.

Up to comparatively recent times there was a steady trade in England for the Iceland pony, many going to work in the pits, others finding themselves between the shafts working mostly in the towns. From the description given here of these small, sturdy ponies it will be correctly assumed that they gave very great satisfaction, and even today one hears the wish expressed that some Icelanders could be seen as in the old days. The student of the pony will note the close resemblance in outline, conformation and colour to many of the northern pony breeds—Scandinavian, Highland, Norwegian and, to a lesser extent, the Shetland and Connemara. In that group are gathered ponies which excel in a toughness rarely to be found elsewhere, certainly never to be exceeded.

IOMUD

Russia has a number of different breeds and types of horses and ponies, at least fourteen, which is not surprising considering its vast territory. Nonetheless we find at times one breed intermingling with another, or some which are produced by tribal selection, such as the Iomud.

Owing to its remoteness, and contrary to what we find so frequently in almost every horsebreeding country throughout the world, the admixture of thoroughbred blood is little found in Russia. Naturally it is only when we find a horse having rather more quality that thoroughbred or more likely Arab blood is found, as in Strelets (q.v.).

The Iomud horses are descended from the same ancient taproot as the Akhal-Teke breed, but have been evolved by another Turkoman tribe, the " Iomud. " They differ from the Akhal-Teke (q.v.) in being smaller, not so fast, and they are much more fiery and highly strung. They are run in troops on the plains of Northern Turkmeina, and have great powers of endurance, being able to withstand extremes of temperature ranging from fierce summer heat to the rigours of the severest winters. The Akhal-Teke have been used with success on some Iomud horses which were not up to the high standard desired, and this with excellent results, and it is recorded that both breeds compete together in races and endurance tests.

Italy was never a horse-breeding country of any great note, although it was said that at one time many thousands of almost pure-bred Arabs and Barbs were kept by Pope Gregory the Great at the expense of the State. In the 16th and 17th centuries, in the district of Naples, there was established a Neapolitan breed which became quite famous, the great role in the foundation of this breed being played by Spanish horses

It is interesting to read in Lady Apsley's book " Bridleways Through History " : " Henry VIII undoubtedly imported some Neapolitan stallions " and, more important still, some mares " perfect in shape and size," sent to him by Francisco Gonzaga, Marquis of Mantua, who bred horses at Mormolata on Lake Mincio, and whose

" race " was of such renown that England and France competed for them. Blundeville mentions the " Neapolitan and the Sardinian," which from

their gentle nature and docility, their comely shape, their courage, their sure-footmanship, their well reining, their lofty pace, their clean trotting, their strong galloping and their swift running, they excel numbers of other races, even so far as the fair greyhound the foul mastiff curs.

It is said that the Neapolitan horses were similar to the famous Spanish jennets but bigger, and with paces similar to their Moorish contemporaries in Northern Africa. The Neapolitans were said to take longer to mature than horses of other races, being best when put into training when six or seven years old, and they maintained their perfection considerably longer than other horses.

Since the middle of the 18th century horse-breeding in Italy was very much neglected, and was only revived to some extent during the Fascist regime. According to V. de Simone, " L'ippicultura italiana," 1942, in the province of Belzano, where the Hafflinger Stud Books were established in 1932, the Hafflinger is very popular and also used for the improvement of horses in the mountainous regions of Parma, Piacenza and Como. In Le Murge a large, robust Murgese horse, which is of oriental origin, is bred and much improved by careful selection. In Apulia local mares are bred to Salerno and Maremma stallions with an admixture of English Thoroughbred blood carefully added, thus resulting in strong saddle and draught horses having a good appearance and excellent conformation.

It should be noted that the island of Sardinia produces a pony of considerable worth, which in appearance is very similar to the Corsica ponies. They are bred in a semi-wild state and are very hardy. They stand approximately 13 to 14 hands, are bay in colour, and when exported usually fetch good prices. They are used both for harness work and riding. Heavy cart-horses are seen mostly in the Po Valley and are usually not bred in Italy, as all heavy work in that country is carried on by bullocks and mules. Other very good horses are the Sicilians, which are of Arab type with Spanish and Italian influence.

It should be mentioned that just previous to the Second World War Italy achieved great success in breeding racehorses, an outstanding example being the very well-known and successful " Nearco," sire of " Dante," and another well-known and fashionable stallion, " Donatello II."

Lying as Italy does so much to the southern-most part of Europe, it is surprising to find that the strong, cold-blooded draught horse exists and thrives there, for the tendency is for the lighter or hot-blooded types to predominate in such regions.

It is well known that Italy has produced horse-men of outstanding reputations, not only as instructors in equitation, but also in show jump-ing, and their horse shows are among the best organised in the world. It seems, however—and indeed this applies to some other nations as well—that they must rely to some extent on the imported horses for their requirements. In this connection it should be noted that the show jumper is not a breed, and that all horses, whether pure-bred or cross-bred, are potential show jumpers.

KABARDA : KARABAIR and LOKAI

KABARDA

These horses are found in the mountainous regions of the Caucasus, and are the result of crossing the native Mongol stock with Eastern sires of Persian or Arab blood. They are used both for saddle and pack work, and are exceptionally agile and sure-footed. They are now bred by " selfing, " and breed mostly true to type, but occasional horses deviating from the pure Kabarda type are crossed with English Thoroughbred and Arab sires with good results. They are strong, rather " harnessy " horses, with a distinctly convex profile, and mostly bay in colour without white markings.

Bred amongst mountains, the Kabarda horses are extremely sure-footed, and will ford dangerous rivers and cross precipitous ranges with great courage and sagacity, while their rugged independence is very marked.

KARABAIR and LOKAI

Both these breeds are of mixed Mongol and Arab blood, and owing to the wide pastures of their habitat, Uzbekistan, they have developed into fine horses of two distinct types ; a light saddle or pack horse of good conformation which is bred in the mountainous regions of Uzbekistan, and a heavier harness-type in the valleys and foothills. The national game of " goat-snatching " —in which one mounted man carries a goat while others try to take it from him in full gallop—has developed in both breeds an exceptional agility and speed, while retaining a most tractable nature

This beautiful breed is found in the Caucasian districts, and has greatly contributed in the past to the improvement of the Don horses (q.v.). They are similar to the highest class of Persian horse, that is to say they are predominantly Arabian in conformation, and with the dished face of the Arab as opposed to the straight profile of the Persian. Their characteristic golden colour is to be found nowhere else save in one other Russian breed, the Akhal-Teke (q.v.). This most admired colour, together with admirable conformation, makes the Karabakh breed one of the most beautiful in the world.

In the Siwaliks, the southern foothills of the Himalaya, a number of species of ancient animals have been found, among them being one identical with the British horse, so the Thoroughbred and the Indian country-bred both may have a remote common ancestor in the horse of the Siwaliks, though they would hardly speak to each other now. The latter is, of course, found all over India, but mostly in the hard, dry, northern plains from the Indus to the Ganges and south to the Deccan. He is generally a wretched little creature, thin, weedy, very narrow, his front legs " coming out of the same hole," as the saying goes, seldom more than 13 to 13½ hands high, but with feet and legs of cast iron, amazing toughness and powers of endurance and the ability to live on next to nothing. Contrary to popular opinion, the Indian has always been a bad horsemaster and an indifferent horseman.

A number of different varieties have developed, usually from the admixture of foreign stock, the most important and well known of them being the Kathiawari and the Marwari, which being very similar in ancestry and characteristics can be taken together. Mention should first be made, however, of the Unmol (meaning " priceless "), varieties of which were bred in the northern Punjab. They are traditionally supposed to be descended from horses brought by Alexander the Great when he invaded India, and are described as being very strong, elegant and shapely, with a long mane and compact body. The pure breed, however, is now practically extinct, those that are still maintained by local maliks being well mixed with imported Thoroughbred and Arab blood. The Kathiawari takes its name from the peninsula of Kathiwar on the north-west coast of India between the Gulfs of Cutch and Cambay. The common ancestors of the Kathiawari and the Marwari (which is found in Rajputana) are said to be a shipload of Arab horses which was wrecked on the west coast of India. These horses ran wild in the jungles and plains of Kathiawar and Marwar, and naturally mixed with the indigenous " country-bred " pony. The Arab strain certainly shows itself in the best of both these breeds, which have also special characteristics of their own, the inward pointing of the tips of the ears, which almost meet, and the prevalence of sickle hocks. They run from 14 to 15 hands, and the most usual colours are chestnut, brown, bay, grey, piebald and skewbald, with some creams. The best bred of the Kathiawaris are in demand for racing, and in the days of height limits were used for polo. It is not improbable that one of the colleagues of Kipling's " Maltese Cat " was a Kathiawari. Studs of these animals are maintained at Palitana and by the Nawab of Junagarh.

The Marwari figures prominently as a war horse in the annals of Rajasthan, and in the Middle Ages horse-breeding was the chief occupation in Marwar. Ain-i-Akbari mentions that the entire Rajput population of this region formed an imperial service cavalry of over 50,000 horses. Attempts to improve this breed have been made by the Maharaja of Jodhpur.

Like all " country-breds " they are tough and hardy, possessing considerable staying powers and having an easy gait, and, be it said, an uncertain temper.

As neither of these two breeds had been used extensively by the British for polo or any other purpose for a number of years previously, it cannot be said that the withdrawal of the British Army can have had any particular effect on the numbers of ponies bred. Having regard to the wild nature of the country which is their habitat and the primitive agricultural needs of the natives, it may well be that these ponies will hold their own as well as any in these present times, when the horse and pony population of the world is ever decreasing.

If this proves to be the case, it may happen that some grading-up by the introduction of " foreign " blood may take place, as it has in the past.

KLEPPER

The Kleppers are supposed to descend from native mares of the Baltic provinces of Livonia, Esthonia and of the islands of Dago and Oesel which were crossed with Eastern horses. Standing from 13 to 15 hands, they have a good outlook, possess great strength and endurance and some of them show great ability in trotting.

In considering this breed it is as well to bear in mind that by the admixture of alien blood from time to time, and influenced also by soil and climate, several variations of the breed have been evolved, each bearing its own name. None the less, all have retained a certain similarity and each one is stamped with the characteristics of the original wild horse. In consequence the ability of the Klepper, or of any of its associate breeds, to exist on the most meagre rations, their hardiness and their abnormal strength for size are very pronounced. Their prepotency in stamping their type on their progeny is perhaps second only to that of the Arab, and, despite their normally grim and rigorous existence, they are noted for having exceptionally long lives.

Reference has been made elsewhere to the colours characteristic of the North European breeds and to the fact that so many of them are dun, with the eel-stripe through the back to the tail, with the mane and tail black. With these breeds is included the Klepper, and there is little doubt that the breed can to some extent be classed as one of the great family, with many so different in type, that runs through all the northern regions.

Finnish blood introduced to these Kleppers produced the Viatka pony, 13 to 14 hands, and of two types—Obvinka and Kazanka; all are of good conformation and looks, strong, hardy and fast.

KNABSTRUP

This breed is an old Danish one, exclusively confined to spotted horses, and it seems that the peculiar form of these spots, described by the British Spotted Horse Society as " leopard," " snowflake " and " blanket," are to be found in the Knabstrup.

During the Napoleonic wars, Spanish troops were stationed in Denmark for a short period, and one of their officers left behind a spotted mare, which, although relegated to the honest work required by a butcher in the delivery of meat, proved outstanding both as to speed and endurance. A Major Villars Lunn, the owner of an estate known as Knabstrup, subsequently bought this chestnut mare, which had "blanket" markings with a white mane and tail and was of English hunter rather than of Spanish type. This officer and his father before him were great breeders of horses of riding type, always laying special stress on hardiness, speed and endurance, their stock originating from the famous old Royal Frederiksborg stud which was of Spanish-Arab-Barb type similar to the Lippizan.

So it was that the butcher's mare, which was named Flaebehoppen, became the foundation mare of the spotted Knabstrup breed. In 1812 she was put to a Frederiksborg stallion of Palomino colour and produced a colt Flaebehingsten, which became the foundation stallion of the breed, and he, too, had similar colouring and the markings of the original mare. It is said that this horse, while having similar colourings which were of lighter shades, had a general and rather peculiar metallic appearance and was described as having " more than twenty colours."

In Denmark, interest in this breed is very considerable, more than one Society having been formed, and there are a number of stud farms in the country.

The picture shown is of a stallion, Silverking II, being " leopard " with black spots. Needless to say, with the inevitable variations which occur in all spotted markings, the Knabstrup is sought as a circus horse and may be seen performing in Great Britain. A direct descendant of Silverking, a chestnut blanket filly with white mane and tail, was recently shipped to England.

KONIK (Poland)

There are several native breeds of pony in Poland which go under the general name of *konik* (meaning " small horse "). These all have their own names : Hucul, Žmudzin, Bilgoraj Konik, and many others. The Bilgoraj Konik, in particular, is said to be a direct descendant of wild horses. According to Professor Janikowski in an article on the " Wild Horse of Poland " published in " Nature," 1942 :

His ancestors lived in a wild state in the great forest of Bialowieza in Poland until the eighteenth century, when some of them were brought into a private zoological park near Bilgoraj, belonging to Count Zamoyski. One winter at the beginning of the nineteenth century, when the cold was uncommonly severe, the horses, until then living free, were captured and distributed among the peasants of the neighbouring villages, by whom they were tamed and cross-bred with the local mouse-grey peasant ponies ; though a considerable number of them retained the pure blood of their wild ancestors.

In 1936 attempts were made by Professor Vetulani of Poznan University to breed the forest horse back to its original wild state. The great forest of Bialowieza was made into a national park, and among the animals brought back there were a stallion, " Tref," and a mare, " Czajka," both of which had the remarkable property, possessed by certain other animals, such as the hare, grouse, etc., of turning white in winter, a characteristic unusual in the horse. Every winter they changed their mouse-grey summer coats, with the black dorsal stripes, into white coats, only the face, fetlocks, mane and tail retaining the normal dark colour. After three years of breeding there were eighteen horses in the park at Bialowieza, of which eight had been born in the forest. Some of these inherited the characteristic of changing from a summer to a winter coat. The same Professor Vetulani asserts that the wild horse, described by Herodotus as grazing in the northern marshy land may well have been this Polish wild pony grazing in the Polesie bogs situated close to the Bialowieza Forest.

Apart from the Konik, the greater proportion of the Polish peasant horses belong to the type of Mierzyn, which means a medium horse between two sizes, usually 13 to 14 hands. The small size, as in all these native pony breeds, is more than compensated by their outstanding qualities of hardiness, endurance, ability to live on next to nothing, vitality and great fertility, which they always transmit unimpaired to their progeny. Both the Konik and his cousin the Mierzyn are remarkably long-lived, and capable of work up to a considerable age. It is quite common in Poland to see a 25-year-old pony still able to work.

In the Baltic states also there is a very popular horse called the " Konik horse of the trotter type," which is, in fact, a working horse. It is derived from a small native horse graded-up during many generations by trotter stallions. This breed represents a medium-sized, tough and good-tempered working horse, and is held in high esteem for its hardiness, endurance, speed and unexacting food requirements. In short, their virtues are the result of their vigorous upbringing in severe climatic conditions.

LIMOUSIN

Limousin is a half-bred horse of English blood, and its name is derived from the region where it was bred. It is a big-boned animal standing very often 17 hands and representing the type of heavy hunter. It is able to carry a big weight and can gallop and jump. The horse reaches full development very late, and can hardly be expected to work as a hunter before it is seven years old. Today his breeding is almost given up, as farmers of this region would rather have bullocks of the local breed and of the same name.

For similar purposes there is the Charolais horse, which is also a half-bred horse, but smaller (15 to 16 hands) and lighter than the Limousin.

In considering both the Limousin and the Charolais it must be borne in mind that they share with the famous Anglo-Norman the English Thoroughbred as their foundation sire, and are referred to in their country of origin as being of *Demi sang du Centre*. The reader therefore is referred to the Anglo-Norman, and it is useful to glance also at that other well-known horse of French breeding, the Tarbenian, which is described as being of *Demi sang du Midi*.

When one considers the long-standing reputation of all the breeds above mentioned, one can only hope that they will be retained and fostered. As a nation the French have always shown great skill in the breeding of horses.

This famous breed is of Austrian origin, and takes its name from the place, Lippiza, where the stud farm of the same name was founded in 1580 by the Archduke Charles, son of the Emperor Ferdinand I.

The origin of this breed goes back to 1564, when there had been introduced into Austria a highly specialised type of horse, the Kladruber (taking its name from the stud farm of Kladrub in Bohemia), which was the result of a mixture of Spanish and Neapolitan blood. The characteristics of this breed were a heavy, big-boned frame, small head, round nose, curved or arched neck, and often drooping ears. The height was from 16 to 17 hands. They were bred for court use, to draw the royal carriages and to be ridden in processions and on state occasions. Owing to inbreeding they developed a number of defects, becoming very short-lived, liable to have poor feet and legs not strong enough for their size and weight. In spite of this, however, they continued in use until the break-up of the Austrian Empire in 1918, when they were all sold and dispersed.

The Lippizana is derived from a cross between the Kladruber and a small Italian horse of northern Italy—especially near Trieste and in Gorizia—with a later admixture of Arab blood. These are the animals which were used in the Spanish Riding School at Vienna, which was built for the Emperor Charles VI in 1735 by the architect Fischer von Erlach. It may be noted that the celebrated airs and exercises taught and practised there are not of Spanish origin, in spite of the name of the school, but were initiated by two great horsemen of the past, one English, the Duke of Newcastle, author of "A New Method of Feeding, Dressing and Training Horses," and the other French, Antonius de Pluvinel, riding-master to Louis XIII and author of "Instruction of the King in the Art of Riding."

The Lippizana is a very beautiful horse, nearly always grey. It is extremely shapely and elegant in appearance, with a longish body, well ribbed-up, strong quarters, rather heavy shoulders and neck, small head, good legs with plenty of bone. The nostrils are rather narrow, the eyes large and horizontal. The best of them show their Arab blood, and the general impression is one of strength and grace and dignity. They are intelligent and very docile in disposition. By contrast with their ancestor, the Kladruber, Lippizanas are long-lived, and their intensive training in high school work does not really begin until they are from five to seven years old.

Up to the Second World War the chief breeding-place of this breed was at the Hungarian State Stud at Babolna, which was founded in 1789, when Hungary was part of the Austrian Empire. Breeding was carried on there, on a large scale, of Arabs and half-bred Arabs as well as of Lippizanas. The general system was to breed from selected fillies on their reaching four years. After the first foaling the fillies were broken-in for driving, and those with the best performance continued as brood mares. Apart from his high school use the Lippizana is a magnificent carriage-horse and a good hunter and hack.

Since it has so much presence, especially under saddle, with its spectacular action and arresting colouring, not to mention its understanding nature and tractability, it is somewhat surprising that the Lippizana has not been used even in the now rather distant past as a riding-horse in England.

So great is the reputation of the Lippizana and so world-wide the knowledge of its association with the Spanish Riding School at Vienna, that little more need be said. Long after many types or breeds of note have ceased to exist, the probability is that the Lippizana will be found displaying the traditional acts of the Spanish Riding School as it has done for over three centuries. It is a matter of great satisfaction that the famous Spanish Riding School at Vienna is now re-established.

The Manipur Pony takes its name from the state of that name in Assam where it has been bred from time immemorial. Doubts to the contrary notwithstanding, its claim to be a distinct breed is supported by historical evidence as well as by its appearance. Early manuscripts record that the breed existed at least as far back as the 7th century, when the reigning king of Manipur introduced the game of polo, played on ponies bred in his state.

Major-General Sir James Johnstone, in " My Experience in Manipur and the Naga Hills " (1896), writes :

Manipur in olden days possessed a famous breed of ponies, larger and better bred than the so-called Burmese ponies that came from the Shan States. On these ponies were mounted the formidable cavalry that in the last century made Manipur feared throughout Upper Burma and enabled her rulers on more than one occasion to carry their victorious arms within sight of Ava, where their Raja Pamheita erected a stone pillar to commemorate the event.

It is quite probable that descendants of these same ponies accompanied yet another victorious army, the illustrious 14th, into Burma in 1945 ; for they were used, and valued, as military transport ponies in that most difficult of all battle-grounds.

From the general appearance of the breed it is reasonable to trace its descent from the Mongolian pony on the one hand, the influence of which is noticeable over most of east and south-east Asia, and from Arab blood on the other. And it is probable, too, that they do have some affinity, on that account, with the Shan ponies of Upper Burma. " These two ponies," wrote Captain M. H. Hayes, " appear to belong to a distinct breed, which seems to have no relationship with ponies of any other country except possibly those of Sumatra and Java."

The following description is taken from " Indian Farming," August 1942 :

Though small in size, the animal possesses a proportionate body and is sturdy and sure-footed. The head is smart and carried well-up on a clean, strong, muscular neck. The face is fairly long and exhibits an alert, gentle appearance. The muzzle is fairly broad with well-dilated nostrils. The chest is broad and the ribs amply sprung. The legs are proportionate in size and of fine quality. Knees and hocks are strong, the shanks clean and straight, and the pasterns possess a gradual and proportionate slope. The animal measures 11 to 13 hands in height and the body-weight is about 650 lb.

MECKLENBURG

The prime object of German horse-breeding was to produce the type of horse which could serve first for military purposes and in peace-time could be useful as a working animal. Thus, besides a few breeds of " cold-blood " horses like the Rhenish or one-time Mecklenburg, which during wars served as heavy artillery horses, many " warm-blood " breeds were artificially created, such as East Prussian, Hanoverian, Holstein and others, which would answer all military requirements. They represent the cavalry or light-draught type of horse, standing from 15·2 to 16·3 hands, with good bone, being good weight carriers with easy action.

Today, the Mecklenburg horse is a " warm-blood " horse got by " warm-blood " stallions out of " warm-blood " mares and bred by breeders organised as " The Association of Mecklenburg Warm-blood Breeders." The Mecklenburg horse passed through several stages. Once a heavy type of horse, in the middle of the 19th century it represented a good saddle-horse which was, unfortunately, very much deteriorated by the introduction and bad management of the English Thoroughbred. With its excellent pastures, Mecklenburg is used not only as the breeding country for " warm-blood " horses, but also as a rearing ground for the 3,000 or so Hanoverian foals which are taken there each year.

Reviewing the position as described, it will be seen that the Mecklenburg, like so many of the German breeds, has passed through many stages as the result of endeavours made to improve the breed by upgrading, coupled with the desire to effect a certain standard or type. Like so many of the country's equine products, the Mecklenburg shows admirable substance and bone. Since in the past the object has been to breed a general-purposes horse, with a strong emphasis on one suitable for cavalry or artillery, it is a matter for conjecture what future type will be evolved by Germany, in view of the almost complete mechanisation of the Army. It may be that with such excellent pasturage the country may concentrate on producing a riding-horse which, as has been shown, would not be foreign to the Mecklenburg breed.

MONGOLIAN

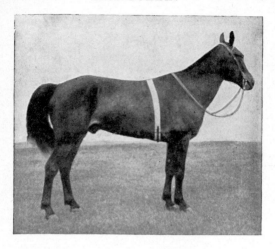

This horse, or rather pony, among the most ancient of the types of *Equus caballus*, is to be found, both domesticated and feral, all over Mongolia, that vast, desolate area reaching from Manchuria in the east to Turkestan in the west, bounded by Siberia on the north and by Tibet and China to the south. These ponies are exceedingly plentiful, being kept and bred in huge numbers by the Buriats and other Mongolian tribes, and, as may be expected in this inhospitable region, are extremely hardy and enduring.

In the eastern parts of Mongolia they are much in demand for export to China for racing and polo. There they are also crossed with other imported foreign breeds, from which has been produced the so-called China pony (illustrated above), which is not really a breed at all. In the west, Mongolian ponies have undoubtedly mingled in the past with Arabs to produce the Turkoman horses of Turkestan. To the south in Tibet and in the Himalayas their influence is also seen in the hill ponies of those regions, Spiti, Bhutan, Yarkand, and so on, which are all certainly closely related to the Mongolian. Nor does its influence end there. The animals of Burma and Malaya are not indigenous to those countries, and there is no doubt that they derive in part from Mongolian stock. Even the famous Manipur breed has its ultimate origin from it.

The nomad owners of these ponies, while they breed them in large numbers, do not take any special pains to improve the stock, and certainly do not waste any time or money on feeding. The pony has to live on whatever it can pick up, which is not much and is tough at that. Consequently the teeth are usually very much worn down. Stallions are always animals selected by the breeders, but no attention is paid to the mares.

The average height of the Mongolian stallion is about 13·1 hands, but varies between 12·2 and 13·3 hands. The lowest heights seem to be found usually to the east along the China border, and the best in the northern districts.

In appearance they have heavy heads and shoulders and smallish eyes, thick necks, deep chests, well-sprung ribs, good quarters and loins and legs, with plenty of bone. Their hoofs are iron hard, though they are apt to be abnormally worn down by the hard and stony going. Mane and crest are coarse, coats long and shaggy, with flowing forelocks and tails that sweep the ground. The tails are thick-haired at the roots.

MORGAN

This American breed of light horse sprang
literally from one progenitor, the little bay
stallion " Justin Morgan," which was foaled in
1793 in the Green Mountain country of Vermont,
U.S.A. Little is known of the origin of this horse,
except that his ancestry must have been mainly
Thoroughbred or Arabian.

By a lucky chance his owner, Thomas J.
Morgan, impressed by his looks decided to try
him at stud before having him gelded. The
results were striking. Although put to ordinary
mares his progeny were almost exact replicas of
himself. His fame soon spread, and mares were

sent to him from all over the country. He was eventually bought by the U.S. Army for a very large sum, and a Morgan Stud Farm was established in Woodstock, Vermont. So he remained at stud all his life, producing a breed almost unique in its uniform excellence and trueness to the original type. And not only did " Justin Morgan " reproduce himself with astonishing uniformity, but he stamped himself on his stock with such strength that his own type was produced and reproduced with unfailing regularity from generation to generation. " Justin Morgan " died in 1821, but his breed remained the most popular and valuable of American general-purpose animals until ousted to some extent by the Standard Bred (q.v.), which, however, owes many of its best features to the older breed. In addition he has left his imprint on most of the American breeds, the Standard Bred (Trotter and Pacer), the American Saddle Horse, and the Tennessee Walking Horse all owing something to him.

We can best give the characteristics of this breed by describing its ancestor. " Justin Morgan " was only 14 hands high. He was a bay, with black points and a small star. He was a compact, extraordinarily solidly built horse, very muscular, with powerful shoulders, thick neck and crest, and shapely legs and feet. He had a thick, heavy mane and tail, and long, shaggy fetlocks, the only characteristics which succeeding generations have modified. The height of the breed now varies between 14 and 15 hands, and the weight from 800 to 1,000 lb. The most usual colours are bay, brown, black and chestnut. Breeding is now carried on mainly under United States Government supervision.

Breed Society : Morgan Horse Club.

MUSTANG (BRONCO)

The term " Mustang " was applied primarily to the feral or semi-feral horses of the plains of western America, but has been extended to include the herds on the pampas of South America as well. The derivation of the word is from the Spanish *mestengo*, meaning " stranger," which in turn comes from the Spanish *mesta*, the name given to associations of graziers, one of whose functions was the appropriation of wild cattle which had attached themselves to the tame herds.

Like the word, the horse in historic times in America is of Spanish origin, and the animals which Cortez brought over from Cuba in 1519 were the first true horses ever to be seen in the New World. When the " caballeros " of Cortez charged them, the Aztecs thought the gods had come down to earth, and fled in terror ; and it is no exaggeration to say that without the horse

Cortez could not have conquered Mexico or Pizarro, later, Peru. Other horses were introduced later by the Spaniards into Florida, by Ponce de Leon and by De Soto, Coronado and others, into the unknown hinterland of North America west of the Mississippi, becoming in due course Texas, Arizona, Colorado, etc. There is a complete list of the horses of Cortez, which indicates that these, and by inference the later importations, were of Spanish blood, going back to Saracen (Arabian and Barb) ancestry.

During the adventures and misadventures of the *conquistadores*, many of their horses strayed or were captured by the Indians, and it is from them there grew, multiplying in a surprising manner in the three centuries up to 1819 (less than a hundred generations), the vast herds of feral and half-tamed horses which roamed the great plains at the beginning of the American pioneering times, and which made the Red Indian the superb natural horseman that he was and is. To all these animals the comprehensive name of Mustang is given. There were various types within this term, the best being that known as the Indian Pony, a product of Indian breeding and selection. The term " Bronco " (from the Spanish word meaning rough and rude), originally applied to the wildest and most untameable Mustangs—hence the phrase " Bronco-busting " —has now come to apply to all these types equally with Mustangs.

The original Mustang was a small horse, seldom more than 14·2 hands in height and from 600 to 800 lb. in weight. In common with all these small utility breeds, whether in the East or in the West, they were nothing much to look at, scraggy and rough, of uncertain temper, but hardy and courageous, and apparently built of cast iron. Occasional throwbacks to their original remote Arabian ancestry were known to appear, becoming legendary figures for their outstanding size, beauty and speed. Every known colour was represented and many strange shades and combinations, of which again only the East has the like to show. Once broken and domesticated the Mustang was a useful light saddle-horse, and was the original cow pony.

Today the true Mustang has been largely succeeded by the modern range horse, the result of the crossing of a diversity of strains—Thoroughbred, Standard, Morgan, Quarter, and others. Though this may be true as a general statement the plain-looking and rough and workmanlike horse of the true Mustang type *does* still exist, remaining the useful, if at times very wild, servant he always was, and it is good to feel that this is so, thus retaining the old-time romance of the Wild West. By no manner of means is the cowboy of today mounted on beautiful Palominos, or flashly-marked Pintos, as American films would often have us believe. It is worth noting here in connection with cow-ponies that the Arab on account of the soundness of its legs, is increasingly used for cutting-out cows on the ranch.

The Mustang has figured much in the annals of the plains, and certainly in fiction and film. Because of this a certain romance has been built around the breed, and it is to be hoped that its existence will justify a continuance of this.

Of Britain's nine mountain and moorland breeds, the New Forest Pony is, with the exception of the Highland, the largest. Its ancestry, as in the case of the other breeds, is uncertain, and based largely on conjecture, although in the days of Canute mention is made of wild horses living in the Forest. That such have existed continuously since those days there can be no doubt.

Today the New Forest Pony is allowed to roam at will over some 60,000 acres of forest in Hampshire, though in fact there is little to denote a forest, for the land is mostly bare of trees and offers the poorest pasture to the ponies, consisting in the main of heather and poor or rank grass. This has much effect on them, causing them to be hardy and economical feeders when brought off the Forest to " family " life. The breed has been subject to a considerable amount of " improving " by various breeds, and Queen Victoria in 1852 lent an Arab stallion, " Zorah," which was in the Forest for eight years. Not for a decade and more have alien stallions been turned out there, and the pony is now of a definite type, and increasingly, it would appear, breeds true to it.

The New Forest Pony Breeding and Cattle Society do not lay down any official standards for the pony. They may be, however, of any colour, but bays and browns predominate ; in height they vary from 12 to 14 hands. They have a fairly large but somewhat Eastern type of head, rather a short neck, drooping and rather narrow quarters, but good shoulders and great depth through the heart. They are also narrow and, being used to picking their way over rough ground, have good action and are consequently very surefooted. Accustomed to seeing the traffic along the roads on the verges of which they constantly graze, they become immune to every kind of road terror and make the safest possible mount for children when properly broken-in.

The New Forest Pony, as with other native breeds, plays a most important part as foundation stock. Bred to survive the constant struggle for existence, they develop an acute sense of intelligence, courage and resource. The poor quality of the grazing and the fact of living out in every kind of weather provides them with constitutions of iron.

Owing to parts of the New Forest being largely a health and pleasure resort, the pony, though running wild, is less shy of mankind than other mountain and moorland breeds, and in consequence, is much in demand as a tractable and dependable riding-pony. Its larger size, moreover, makes it more of a family pony, for it is well up to carrying considerable weight. Very large numbers of these ponies have always been found working in harness in large towns, mostly in Southern England, and as hardy honest workers it would be difficult to find any more suitable for the job.

It is claimed for these ponies that they are extremely easy to break in and, accustomed from the day they are foaled to picking their way across the numerous bogs of the Forest, through high heather and over rabbit warrens, they have a good action—in consequence they make good rides across any kind of country. On account of their docility and friendly bearing they are safe rides for children and, as has been shown, may be classed as suitable " family " ponies.

In no other breed in the groups of Mountain and Moorland ponies of the British Isles has there been shown more improvement in recent years than in the New Forest. In mixed classes at shows the breed may well be standing high in competition with all comers—something which would not have been seen at any time previous to the Second World War. Being usually the second largest of the group, and being more of a true riding type than the larger breed, the pony is in steady demand.

BREED SOCIETY : The New Forest Pony Breeding and Cattle Society.

This attractive pony is one of the most distinctive and most interesting types of the horse in Europe. Actually two types of this breed are recognised, the *fjord-hest* of western Norway and the *doele-hest* or " valley horse " of the interior. Both have the same characteristics, but the ancient original type seems to be the one of the west.

The chief feature of the breed is, of course, the distinctive colour, between cream and dun. A dark dorsal stripe runs from tail to forelock through the mane, which is usually clipped to 4–5 inches to stand up in a fine crest. The legs are dark, and occasionally zebra markings occur. Bays and browns are also found, but dun is the prevailing and ancestral colour.

They are stocky, compact little animals, standing from 14 to 14·2 hands, with thick necks and shoulders, but good shoulders nevertheless, and broad chests. They have short backs with plenty of depth and width of barrel, and strong short legs. The head is of medium size, usually concave, with intelligent eyes, tending towards the horizontal, with rather rounded ears. In their general aspect and colour they show their primitive origin with marked signs of Eastern blood, which make them extremely handsome and striking ponies.

By nature the Norwegian pony is docile and friendly and fond of company. Its pace is akin to a shuffling trot and it has a will of its own, but it is hardworking and tireless. It is used mostly for draught, either in quaint, low carts with four very small wheels or, for passengers, in a species of two-wheeled dogcart or the *Cajol*, which takes two people one behind the other—nevertheless it can be quite a good ride.

The ponies are never clipped and never rugged. In the winter they are housed in communal stables with cattle, pigs and other livestock, and are fed on hay only, unless timber hauling or other specially heavy work is to be done, when they are given oats and bran. Like all other primitive pony types, they can thrive on the shortest and roughest of rations. In the summer they are grass fed by means of tethered grazing.

There is no certainty but much conjecture about the origin of the Norwegian pony. It has been suggested that it has affinity with the Celtic pony of Connemara, the Scottish Highland, and the pony of Iceland, and that they and the Russian tarpan, the now extinct wild or semi-wild horse of the Urals, all come from the same stock ; and there is no doubt that these breeds have many points in common. At the same time it is highly probable that Arab blood was introduced into the Norwegian stock at some very early date in history, though how or when will never be known. Naturalists in general, however, agree that the horses of Norway, and of other parts of Europe of similar type, represent a very ancient species reaching back into prehistoric times in Europe, and that they inherit their distinctive dun hue and shape either directly or by reversion from the wild horse of Mongolia, the ancestral wild horse of Przevalski.

When considering the Norwegian pony the reader is advised to associate its type with all the Northern European ponies, for they have many points in common, so much so that it is remarkable that each breed, Highland, Klepper, Shetland or Swedish, Russian Viatka or Smudish (and include others too), is so very different in appearance. It may be said with some truth that all these breeds are to some extent members of one great family which has, in the course of very many generations, spread itself over many lands, undoubtedly to the great advantage of those they have served.

Though well known to tourists from England the pony is practically unknown now in the British Isles, though in the old days specimens were seen from time to time. Nor would the pony find much favour in these days when the riding-pony is in so much demand and is required to reach a fair standard of refinement, whilst the pony as a draught animal finds almost no market at all. The Norwegian is, however, an unusual and genuinely attractive pony and he would be a welcome resident in this country.

OLDENBURG

The heaviest of the German " warm-blood " breeds is the Oldenburg, which is a big animal, often standing quite 17 hands, with many characteristics of the " cold-blood " horse, such as flat hoofs, heavy heads and necks and flat ribs. Besides these defects very often found in " cold-blood " breeds, the Oldenburg horse has the great quality of early maturity. As a breed it is not a hardy type and is lacking in endurance. Today the Oldenburg has a good deal of English Thoroughbred blood, the introduction of which did not make for improvement, and it can be described as a half-bred horse of heavy type. As such, therefore, and in particular having regard to its early maturity, it is a good commercial proposition.

ORLOV

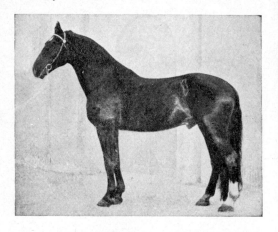

The originator of this famous breed of Russian trotters was Count Alexius Grigorievich Orlov, a Russian nobleman who was born in 1737 and died in 1808. He was renowned for his great strength and dexterity, and was a man of many interests besides the horse. He was concerned with his brother Gregory in the conspiracy of 1762 which led to the deposition and death of Czar Peter III, and was said to have been his actual murderer. He also commanded the Russian fleet which annihilated the Turks at Chesme in 1770. When he died he left 30,000 serfs and an estate worth five million roubles.

After his more violent activities he appears to have turned his attention to horse-breeding, and in 1777 evolved the breed which for ever after was to be known by his name when his other exploits were forgotten. He produced the Orlov Horse by crossing the following bloods : English Thoroughbred, Arab, Dutch, Danish and Mecklenburg. The first stallion was an Arab, called "Smetanka," which was put to a Dutch mare from whom was bred a stallion called "Polkan." The first Trotter out of the latter's progeny was a stallion out of a black Dutch mare which was named "Bars First." This horse is considered to be the head of the Orlov breed. There were later admixtures of Dutch, English and Arab blood.

Trotting has always been a popular sport in Russia, and in pre-Revolution Russia the Orlov breed was developed for that purpose. As it is known now, the breed has two definite lines, a heavy type, which is predominantly black, and a slighter type, with more pronounced Arab features, which is usually grey. The latter has been more successful on the race-track and leads in speed records. So far as is known at present, the fastest mile in Russia has been trotted in 2 minutes 6 seconds, which is still a good way behind the American record of 1 minute 55 seconds. (See Standard Bred.)

A good Orlov is very handsome, with a small head, very Arabian in appearance, broad chest, longish back, good well-rounded quarters and strong muscular legs. The height goes up to 17 hands.

At the beginning of the century the type was becoming a little degenerate, longer in the body and legs, and with decreasing stamina. New colours, dark brown and dark chestnut, also made their appearance. During the Revolution the proletarian zeal of the Bolsheviks extended to thoroughbred horses as well as to human aristocrats, and many were destroyed. Common sense and sporting instinct, however, seem to have prevailed in time, and the breed was saved and is still carried on together with the sport of trotting racing. Count Orlov's stud was acquired by the Czarist State, and under the name of the Khrenovsky Stud was the central breeding place of the Orlov Horse. Before the Revolution there were about 3,000 stud farms in Russia devoted to the breeding of these Orlov Trotters.

This breed is another instance of the Arabian Horse foundation, and it is characteristic of that blood and a mark of its prepotency that the Orlov head still bears the Arab stamp.

The Orlov achieved its greatest fame as a trotter and in the latter half of the last century was looked upon as the supreme horse for that work. With the strong commercial development of the trotting horse for the race-track, mostly in America, by the most careful selection and scientific breeding and feeding, the Orlov could not now compete on equal terms. This is a case of scientific development producing excessive speed to the exclusion of all else, and has its counterpart in the Thoroughbred ousting the Arab from the racecourse and polo ground, to the loss, as many believe, of soundness and stamina. Reference has been made to the 3,000 stud farms in Russia devoted to the breeding of this horse—an almost unbelievable number, by the way—but it is quite impossible to say how many of these still exist today. The least that can be hoped is that this world-famous breed still flourishes.

PALOMINO

The term " Palomino " as applied to this beautiful horse of North America, appropriately known as " the golden horse of the West," is not yet strictly a breed, but a colour. This colour is literally gold, though variations from a soft cream or light blonde chestnut to the darker shades are admissible. At its best the coat has been described as metallic in sheen comparable within a few shades to a United States gold coin. The mane and tail should be very light, almost white, and except for white on the face and legs no other colours or markings are admitted ; albino and pinto parentage are forbidden. The eyes are dark, and blue or chalk eyes are not accepted.

The ultimate origin of this attractive colouring goes back to remote ages, it being mentioned in

171

Homeric times. For practical purposes, however, it appears to be of Spanish origin from Saracen and Moorish stock, and there is no doubt that the type contains Arab and Barb blood. Horses of this colour became highly prized in Spain, and Queen Isabella, the sponsor of Columbus, encouraged their breeding. It is possible that such animals were taken to the West Indies by Columbus, but it is on record that Cortez had them in Mexico in 1519. In Spain these horses were called " Ysabellas " in honour of the famous queen. It is said that they take their present name from one Juan de Palomino, to whom Cortez presented one of them.

They were rediscovered about a hundred years ago when the United States took possession of California in 1848 after the Mexican war. Then Palominos were used extensively as saddle-horses and for parade and spectacular purposes, and also for racing until ousted by the speedier Thorough-bred. Their vogue then declined until recent times, when they were rediscovered and taken up for their appearance and excellent riding qualities.

Apart from the colour the following are the main physical characteristics of the Palomino. General appearance is of Arab or Barb type, only larger and more solid. The height is from 15·2 to 16 hands, and weight from 1,200 to 1,600 lb. Only horses of over 14·2 hands are admitted into the register. For the rest they have the normal points of a good horse, with a fine showy action under saddle, a mild, amenable disposition and good movement.

The breeding is generally a cross between Palomino and light chestnuts of the light horse breeds, and also Palomino to Palomino. A cross between a chestnut mare with light mane and tail and a Palomino stallion will usually produce a Palomino foal in 80 per cent. of such crosses. But the breeding is still in the experimental stage and by no means fixed. Foals are usually true Palomino at birth, with blue eyes. The colour changes somewhat with age, and the eyes darken. Manes and tails start by being chestnut, but whiten with age.

Breeding is from any type of recognised light horse breeds, but the infusion of pony or draught blood is barred. The three main types are the Parade (or Show) type ; the Bridle Path type, a general utility saddle-horse ; and the Stock Horse for range work.

So far as the British Isles is concerned, not until recent years has any effort been made to foster the Palomino, and today the body which is concerned with its future is the British Palomino Horse Society. At varying times classes have been held for them at horse shows and they have appeared in parades. Progress must necessarily be slow, for there are few of these coloured horses in the country, still fewer of true riding type. On the other hand, it is not too optimistic to hope that enthusiastic breeders will be found in some numbers, for there must surely be a good market for a horse which can claim, after all, that where colour is concerned, he stands unbeaten.

BREED SOCIETIES are : The Palomino Horse Association, the Palomino Horse Breeders of America, and the British Palomino Horse Society.

PERCHERON

In the Percheron Horse we have one of the
most popular draught horses to be found at work
today, and its popularity extends far beyond
France, where it originated, for it is to be found
in great numbers not only in Great Britain but
in America, Canada and throughout the British
Dominions. Its many qualities have caused the
breed to spread through many Continental
countries, and of all heavy breeds it is perhaps
the most widely dispersed through the world.

As is the case with so many, it is an admixture,
based probably upon the working horse of
Belgium and Northern France, where a strong,
short-legged and active horse was the type
required. The actual credit for founding the

Percheron Horse is due to a certain number of French farmers who, some hundred years ago, farmed a small area not more than perhaps 60 miles square, the district being known as Le Perche, from which, of course, the horse takes its name. There is no doubt they produced an animal of outstanding qualities.

The horse is of low draught, having a short and compact body of tremendous depth, with quarters of outstanding size. Exceptionally short-legged, the horse carries great bone, and it is surprising that so heavy a horse can be so active, for that is indeed what it is, and it is claimed of the Percheron that for farming work it is a great saver of time in getting to its daily job. The fact that it is a good footed horse may be the result of having been worked on stone block roads ; none but horses of good, hard, blue feet such as those possessed by the Percheron could stand up to that kind of work, and it has, with them, well set joints and flat, flinty bone. The horse, of course, is clean-legged, that is, it is devoid of hair or " feather." Percherons are docile and very easily handled, and because of this they are easy to break, especially if they have been handled as foals, which is of considerable advantage in days when labour is difficult to obtain and so much of it unskilled.

Description. The British Percheron is essentially a heavy-draught horse possessing great muscular development combined with style and activity. Should possess ample bone of good quality, and give a general impression of balance and power. *Colour*, grey or black only, with a minimum of white. Skin and coat of fine quality. *Size*, stallions not less than 16·3 hands and mares not less than 16·1 hands, but width and depth not to be sacrificed to height. *Head*, wide across eyes, which should be full and docile ; ears medium in size and erect ; deep cheek, curved on lower side, not long from eye to nose ; intelligent expression. *Body*, strong neck, not short, stallions full arched crest, wide chest, deep well-laid shoulders ; back strong and short ; ribs wide and deep, deep at flank ; hind-quarters of exceptional width and long from hips to tail, avoiding any suggestion of goose rump. *Limbs*, strong arms and full second thighs, big knees and broad hocks ; heavy flat bone, short canons, pasterns of medium length, feet of reasonable size and good-quality hard blue horn. Limbs as clean and free from hair as possible. *Action*, straight, bold, with a long, free stride rather than short, snappy action. Hocks well flexed and kept close.

Little more need be said of this admirable breed. Its whole future is dependent upon the extent to which the heavy horse survives the onslaught of the internal combustion engine, and it may be that the breed will flourish in some countries (for the Percheron has travelled far afield) and decline in others. In this connection there is little enough evidence for an opinion to be formed as to whether the clean-legged horse (Percheron or Suffolk) has proved to be the *more suitable*, compared with the breeds carrying a heavy growth of hair on heels and legs (Shires and Clydesdales).

BREED SOCIETY : British Percheron Society.

PERSIAN

The tale goes that the Persian horses descending from the tarpan were known as a breed long centuries before Christ. There is a theory which may be liberally discussed that Persian horses were ancestors of the Arabs, which finds a great justification in the looks and many characteristics common to both breeds. We may safely say that the Persian horse was a typical oriental horse of a great beauty, full of quality, high spirited, speedy and courageous, making an excellent war horse, much appreciated by Islam warriors.

Today there are many different breeds in Persia: Persian Arab, the Turkoman horse, Shirazi horse (the Gulf Arab), the Kurdistan pony, the Karadagh, the Bokhara pony, the Yamoote, and some Russian breeds such as Orlov Trotters, etc.

The Pinto, or Painted Horse, of America must be well known to all readers of Wild West stories, and the word, which is of Spanish derivation, has come to be applied to all those queerly marked black-and-white and bay- or brown-and-white horses which we know in this country as piebald and skewbald.

Examples of this peculiar colouring, which is the result of the combined action of albinism (whiteness), melanism (blackness) and erythema (redness) on the skin, are found all over the world and in most breeds of horses, but more especially in the primitive types, so it cannot be said that the Pinto is a breed in the strict sense of the word. It is a fact, however, that horses of this colouration are widely prevalent all over the North and South

American continents, and the modern Pinto is recognised as a distinctive American horse. In recent years a society has been formed in the United States called the Pinto Horse Society, with the general objects of gaining recognition for, and the improvement of, typical Pinto horses and ponies, to study and perpetuate the type, to go in for scientific breeding, and to establish a register of Pinto horses.

There is no doubt that the " painted " horse is most attractive and spectacular to look at, especially if the markings are produced in the best of any of the established types. Horses of this coloration have had a reputation the world over for toughness and endurance, and for that reason, with the added advantage of natural camouflage, were always favourites with the Red Indian as war and ceremonial horses. They are now equally popular with the American riding public, and ranches in Canada and the United States are devoted solely to breeding them.

There are no physical features peculiar to the Pinto, except that most specimens appear to have thick necks and rather heavy shoulders, but the types of marking are interesting. There are two distinct patterns, known as Overo and Tobiana, the names derived from the Spanish, and are used in the Argentine by the Criollo (q.v.) Registry.

In Overo markings the white patches always originate from the belly and extend upwards. The back, mane and tail are generally dark ; dark and white alternate on the legs, which are rarely all white. White faces and glass (blue) eyes are fairly prevalent. There is no fixed rule about the size of the patches.

The Tobiana pattern can be distinguished from the Overo by the fact that it has no regular place of origin, white patches starting often from the back, and that the white and coloured areas are usually larger and nearly always solid rather than patchy. White legs are more often found, but the white face and glass eye are not so frequent. The dark patches in both cases are mostly black, brown and bay. Tobiana horses tend to be larger and heavier than the Overos. There is no limit to the size and shape of the markings, which certainly contribute to the charm and variety of this distinctive type of horse.

Breeding results show that the Pinto strain is very potent and will reproduce itself fairly constantly. Special classes for these horses have been introduced into American shows, and the accepted judging rule is 50 per cent. for markings and 50 per cent. for conformation and performance.

In the days when horse-dealers were found in great numbers in the British Isles, it was claimed by them that they could always sell an " odd-coloured " horse, as it was called. The reason for this was that because of its often strange marking, and the vivid effect caused by the white background, the horse would always draw the attention of the public. In short it was, especially if put to a smart butcher's, baker's or other tradesman's cart, a very good advertisement. That market, and how very great it was, has been lost and will never be recovered. As a hack of the riding school type the horse is in demand but not for hunting, where its colour is looked upon as too noticeable.

POLISH ARAB

The Poles have been renowned through history as great horse-lovers and great horse-breeders, with a pronounced individuality in their methods. One of their great authors wrote once : " Having prayed to God for help, then a horse lover does his best in breeding his horses . . . and trusts more to his own experience than to books." Their horses have always been in great demand throughout Europe, whatever the breed or period, and the Polish cavalry of the 17th century, mounted on the Polish horse as it then existed, was almost invincible.

These horses had Eastern blood in them, Arab, Barb, Turkish, Persian, etc. The Arab, however, played an increasingly important role in Polish horse-breeding, and has held the highest place in the estimation of the Poles since the 16th century, when the Polish Sigismund II (Augustus) was the only European ruler to have a royal stud of pure Arabs at Knyszyn. Arabian horses were, however, certainly introduced earlier than that by capture and tribute during the many wars with the Turks and Tartars.

The oldest Arab studs in Poland are those of Chrestowka and Szamrajowska, belonging to the Sanguszko family. The former, known as the Slawuta Stud, dates from 1506, and was re-organised in 1791 by Jerome Sanguszko, who in 1803 sent the first horse-buying expedition from Europe to Arabia, which returned in 1805 with five stallions and one mare. A second expedition in 1816, which was greatly indebted to an English resident in Aleppo named Rawson, brought back nine fine stallions, of which the best were " Hajlan " and " Dzielf," and one mare.

Other Polish princely families, such as Potocki, Rzewuski, Rozwadowski, also imported Arabs periodically ; and one Polish nobleman, Count Rzewuski, lived in the desert and became a legendary figure among the Bedouins.

The policy of Polish breeding was always to introduce fresh blood into the local stock by regular importations from Arabia. As a result Polish-bred pure Arabs have been in demand all over the world and have taken a high place in all the pre-war international horse shows. Arab studs in the United States, particularly, have been established with imported Polish Arab sires and mares. Among famous prizewinners of the past are " Melpomene," a mare from the Slawuta Stud (Paris 1900), and the famous and subsequent English champion the beautiful " Skrowonek," from the Antoniny Stud.

To the student of good horses and therefore of correct conformation, the Polish Arab left little to be desired. Of a good front, with well set-back shoulders, the horse would in the majority of cases always show a strong-topped, short-backed and deep-set body on short legs. The Arab gave it just that amount of elegance which, combined with the rather stouter material provided by the female side, produced an animal which appealed to all connoisseurs of horses. Furthermore, these were to be found as a level whole in great numbers, a tribute to the genius of the Polish nation as horse-breeders.

BREED SOCIETY : The Arab Horse Breeding Association of Poland.

POLISH HALF-BRED

Apart from racing, the prime purpose of the Polish breeding of Thoroughbreds (*q.v.*) was to improve the native stock and to produce a good half-bred riding and working horse.

The nature of the country—the wide agricultural lands, type of soil, lack of good roads, and distances from railways—rendered the heavy-draught horse, such as the Percheron and Shire, almost useless. The need was for strong, lighter-weight animals of good blood and bone.

In Poland a Half-bred horse is one which has English Thoroughbred, Arab, or Anglo-Arab blood on at least one side of his pedigree. Half-bred stud books or registers are kept, and entry into them is very strictly controlled. It was during the period between the wars that the breeding of Half-breds was reconstructed on a highly selective basis, and some very good types were produced. The requirements of cavalry during that time, of course, played an important part in this development.

The type of Half-bred varies in different provinces of Poland, according to variations of soil, climate, strains of blood, and the local needs. That of the Poznan and Pomeranian provinces was based on the English Thoroughbred and was a big-boned animal of good conformation and action, bred from stallions of the Racot Stud with both local and German (Trakehnen) brood mares. These provinces specialised in producing cavalry remounts. In 1938 the Racot Stud had four Trakehnen stallions, eighty-six brood mares and a hundred young stock.

The Kielce province bred a horse full of quality, and of about 15·2 hands, from Arab stock. The

Lublin Half-bred has English blood; while Warsaw and Lodz provinces produce both English and Anglo-Arab Half-breds.

The dominant factor in the breeding of Half-breds was the army, which bought a large number of horses every year. The specifications, most strictly adhered to, were: medium size, full of quality, near to the ground, well-ribbed, with deep girth, strong legs and good bone, and free action. Good temperament, courage, endurance and ability to " do " well were also essential qualities.

Half-breds were also much used in agriculture, where they proved themselves as useful as in military service. Polish horsemen on Half-breds competed in shows and tests all over Europe, and at the Berlin Olympic Games Poles were the only riders other than the Germans who rode horses bred in their own country.

It is not really possible to compare the Polish Half-bred with the English Part-bred Arabian, since the English product has, so far as the Arab Horse Society's Register is concerned, confined entries to horses and ponies of the riding type, whereas the Polish counterpart has leaned towards producing a not-too-heavy horse for agriculture. It is, moreover, unlikely that the English Society will do the same.

As a general commentary it can be said with assurance that the meticulous care shown by the Polish horse-breeders in producing the Polish Arab has been exemplified in the Polish Half-Bred.

POLISH THOROUGHBRED

By the term " Polish Thoroughbreds " is meant horses of pure English Thoroughbred stock as bred and developed in Poland. The first English Thoroughbreds were introduced into Poland early in the 19th century by four men in particular : Count A. Zamozski, E. Eberhard, F. Ursyn Niemcewicz, and, rather later than the first three but no less prominent, Count Krasinski.

The Polish Horse Racing Association, analogous to the Jockey Club of England, was formed in 1841 ; but breeding racehorses was an expensive hobby, and did not extend beyond the efforts of a few rich families until 1872, when economic conditions improved generally. The introduction of the totalisator to race meetings in 1879 contributed materially to the improved financial conditions and so to the wider development of Polish Thoroughbred breeding.

The most important studs during this period were : L. Grabouski's stud, founded in 1846 at Leczna and later transferred to Serniki ; Jan Ursyn Niemcewicz's, at Stoki in 1850 ; Count L. Krasinski's, at Krasne in 1857 ; Count August Potocki's, at Jablonna in 1866 ; W. W. Mysyrowicz's, at Łoś in 1867 ; Baron L. Kronenburg's, at Brzeź ; Jan and Edward Reszka, at Borowno and Skrzydow in 1883 ; H. Block's, at Leczna in 1893 ; Prince Lubomirski's, at Kruszyna in 1895 ; and Michal Berson's, in Leszno in 1897.

All these studs were of a very high standard, thanks mainly to the good brood mares imported from England, France, Germany and Austria. One of the best known stallions in those days was " Flying Fox," imported from England by

E. Blanc, who paid 37,000 guineas for him. He stood at Jardy at a fee of 10,000 francs.

Thoroughbreds bred in Poland ran with success all over Europe, notably in Russia at Moscow, Petrograd and Tsarskoe Selo, as well as Baden-Baden, Vienna and Hamburg.

In the 'nineties a number of big private stables declined, and were replaced by training stables on English lines, which had in training large numbers of individually owned and bred horses. After 1903 with the death of the great amateur promoters of Thoroughbred breeding, such as Ludwik Grabowski and Count Krasinski, the breeding of racehorses in Poland declined. There was, however, a considerable revival after the First World War, through the efforts of Frederik Juriewicz, who was responsible for saving over 200 Thoroughbreds evacuated to Odessa at the beginning of that war. One of these horses won the " Derby " at Odessa in 1918. In 1919 they were returned safely to Poland via Rumania.

A general description of the Polish Thoroughbred must necessarily be for practical purposes identical with the English Thoroughbred. To what extent the racehorse of Poland will again affect racing in Europe is entirely problematical. As is generally known, the racing Thoroughbred of France not only survived quite successfully the Second World War, but after the lapse of but a very few years from its cessation, was once again competing with the English racehorse with very considerable success, not only in France, but in England itself. What has been said in general commendation of the Polish-Arab and Polish Half-Bred certainly applies to their Thoroughbred.

POLO PONY

The Polo Pony is a type rather than a breed. As long as the game of polo has existed so has the polo pony, ranging in height from about 12 to 13 hands in the 16th century to 15·2 to 16 hands in 1939, and in breed from the mountain ponies of the Himalaya, the *Manipuris* of Assam, to the Thoroughbred and near-Thoroughbred of England, U.S.A. and the Argentine as well as the Arab. All these variations of pony are still played somewhere or other, for the type of pony used depends on the local conditions and state of development of the game, and, though varying in degree, the requirements of the polo pony are practically the same in all cases.

Polo is a very ancient game, having been played in the Far East, from Persia to Japan, for at least 2,000 years, the name being derived from the Tibetan word *pulu*, meaning a ball. The English naturally discovered it when they went to India, and it was brought back to England, and the first match was played at Hounslow in 1869, advertised as " Hockey on Horseback." The height of the ponies was then about 14 hands, which was stabilised by the Hurlingham Club, London, which became the governing body of the game in 1873. The height of the pony steadily rose with the development of the game, was 14·2 hands before the First World War and was unlimited from 1919 onwards.

In the 'nineties of the last century greater interest was taken in the breeding of polo ponies, when various well-known and enthusiastic players in England began to breed from small thorough-bred sires on good foundation *pony* mares selected for *performance* on the polo ground. Their aim was to reproduce an animal based on pure pony blood which would have the quality and stamina of a miniature hunter, but which would be a true bred *pony*, not a small horse.

Sir Humphrey de Trafford's thoroughbred pony " Rosewater " is considered to be the foundation of the modern polo pony, and he had three famous sons: " Sandiway," out of " Cuddington " ; " Lord Polo," out of " Lady Florence " ; and " Hurlingham," out of " Esmeralda." These three were dispersed to various studs and so widely disseminated the blood of " Rosewater."

The absolute criterion of a good polo pony is performance ; any other standard alone is artificial Some of the best polo ponies of the world in any age would never have got a prize in any show-ring. A polo pony has to be able to gallop at full speed, stop in his own length, turn or swing round, and start again at top speed in any direction. He has to be able to half passage at full gallop and to change leading leg at any speed or angle.

The prize characteristics of a polo pony therefore are : long neck, with plenty of room for flexion between the jaw and the junction of neck and head ; good shoulders ; short strong back and well-sprung ribs, with plenty of room for the lungs, elbows well away from the body, exceptionally powerful quarters, and hocks well let down ; and not least a courageous, eager temperament.

The most optimistic supporter of polo in England could hardly have imagined the post-war revival of the game which has taken place. While it is abundantly clear that the pre-war standard of the pony itself has not been reached, any more than the amenities of extreme luxury associated with the game have returned, none the less the number of provincial clubs and private polo grounds opened has given the greatest satisfaction.

It is a quality in humans to strive for better things, and the best, if attainable. Where the difference between playing an indifferent pony and one of first-rate ability is so great, it can be assumed that many newcomers will be constantly acquiring ponies of better quality and higher training, which suggests that the future is favourable.

BREED SOCIETY : The National Pony Society.

    The Rhenish horse comes from the Rhein Province and represents a heavy-draught type of horse. It is a deep, broad horse, very powerful, of good conformation and bone, with quite good action for a heavy horse, and is easily fed. It stands some 16 to 16·2 hands, and is most often sorrel coloured, then sorrel roan and brown and sometimes brown roan. Mane and tail are light. Some half a century or so ago the Germans founded the Rhenish Stud Book, and the sires which established the most successful bloodlines are: " Lothar III," " Albion d'Hor " and " Indien de Biévène."

    This breed may be quoted as another example of a type being developed to meet the requirements of a locality, for it does not differ materially from many other " clean-legged " heavy draught horses. It has a good reputation for character and service

RUSSIAN SADDLE

Besides the excellent breed of Orlov Trotters, there are several other breeds to be mentioned, such as the heavy-draught horse Beetewk, steppe horse of Russia, and the Viatka pony.

Russian saddle-horses, called also the Orlov Rostopchin breed, were formed from crossing the Orlov Trotter with the Rostopchin saddle-horse. The latter was bred from Arabs and English Thoroughbreds about 150 years ago by Count Rostopchin, a great Russian breeder, on his properties at Veronevo, near Moscow, and later in Orel and Veronej. At a later date his studs were bought by the Russian Government, and since then the Rostopchin saddle-horse has been crossed with the Orlov Trotter, giving as the result what is now called the Russian saddle-horse. In the Ukraine there were three breeding-centres of Russian saddle-horse in its pure type, but during the First World War they were looted by the Germans.

Later there were some serious attempts to restore the breed, and not without success. In " Animal Breeding Abstracts," June 1946, A. Sokolov wrote :

It is hoped that the breed will have been restored in twenty to twenty-five years. The breeding plan envisages the creation of complex hybrids having 16/32, 7/32, 4/32, 2/32 and 1/32 blood of Russian saddle-horse, Arab, English Thoroughbred, Don, Russian Trotter and Akhal-Teke breeds respectively. The ultimate aim is to evolve a breed which will have 3/4, 1/8 and 1/6 blood of Russian saddle horse, Arab and English Thoroughbred respectively.

RUSSIAN STEPPE

Steppe horses belong to a group of Mongolian horses descending from Przevalski's horse, and have many varieties. All of them, however, represent the same type of a small horse (13 to 14 hands) with very strong constitutions and rather heavy, ugly heads on ewe necks. Their legs are very short, but strong and muscular, with small, hard hooves, while their thin coats are covered with very rich, coarse hair protecting them from the severity of the Russian climate. They are very hard and resist all kinds of privation, which is the natural result of being bred in the steppes and having to find under the snow only grass or moss to live on. They have great speed and stamina, and are great weight-carriers. A common sight was to see a 15-stone Cossack galloping on a 13-hands pony. One remarkable achievement was the ride of Cossack D. Pieszkow, who covered nearly 6,000 miles in six months' riding on a steppe horse.

In modern times steppe horses have served as saddle-horses for many Mongolian tribes of Russia or as an agricultural horse for peasants. Later, to increase their size, steppe horses of Russia were crossed with English Thoroughbreds giving in the result an animal from 14·1 to 14·3 hands. They are bred on natural pastures. To what extent breeding is maintained today it is impossible to say, for not the smallest amount of information seems available. For the time being the breed, so far as England is concerned, must exist only as a memory of an outstanding example of the very toughest kind of horse.

This term includes the " Fjord Horse " of Norway, the Gudbrandsdal, another Norwegian indigenous breed which have already been dealt with, and the native ponies of Sweden, Finland and the Baltic States.

In appearance and ancestry, so far as is known, they belong to that group of horses comprising the ponies of the British Isles and North-west Europe generally, deriving from what Professor Cossor Ewart has called *Equus celticus*. At the time when extensive animal migration seems to have been in progress, the British Isles were joined to Europe by land, which tends to support the idea of common origin.

The Finnish horse of today is of medium size, very agile and nimble-footed, with great staying power and toughness of constitution, good, hard feet and strong legs, body thick and muscular. It is mainly used for draught in either wheeled carts or sleighs.

The Swedish horse, according to R. Bolin in " Contribution to the Knowledge of the Origin of the Horse in Sweden," was originally introduced into the country from the Baltic regions from a type supposed to have originated in the Ukraine. There have been found in Sweden the neck vertebrae of a prehistoric horse identical with the Russian tarpan. Besides this native animal, which varies very little from the Finnish pony, there are various cultivated breeds in Sweden which are considered separately.

Historically horses are not mentioned in Sweden until the 6th century, by which time the Swedes were renowned for their horses. Generally the horse appears late in Scandinavia, as may be gathered from their mythology. Thor, the most ancient of the northern gods, is never shown on horseback or in a chariot; the later deities, however, have taken to the horse, Odin on his eight-legged grey "Sleipnir," Heimdal on a yellow-maned horse.

In Norway, in addition to the horse of the Fjords, there is an original type of island horse known as the Gudbrandsdal, which was well-known in North Europe and has been one of the past founders of the modern Swedish breeds. He is a larger animal than the Fjord horse and a good riding horse too.

In the Baltic States are horses of the same primitive types, notably the small Esthonian or Smudish (Zmudzin), the Zemaitukas (q.v.). A Baltic derivative of these types is the Pange, which is a cross between native mares and trotter stallions, and is very popular as a riding and working horse. It ranges between 14 and 15 hands high, and has all the tough, enduring qualities of its ancient forbears, together with good temper and speed.

In reviewing this breed it is well to have in mind what has been written of the Fjord, the Gudbrandsdal and indeed any and all of the North European breeds, because of their close affinity, and in the main their original tap-root. Just as the tropical and semi-tropical climates have produced the "hot-blood" type of horse, as exemplified by the Arab, so the cold northern climates have evolved the "cold-blood" breeds such as that now described.

SCHLESWIG

This horse is bred on the abundant pastures of the western part of Schleswig Province, and is a heavy type of horse, the breeding of which claims a long tradition. In the Middle Ages it was much appreciated, as well as the Fresian, as a saddle-horse to carry heavy armoured knights. Since that time its breeding has been well patronised by German rulers. At the end of the 19th century the Schleswig Horse Breeders Association was organised to control its breeding and breed a type of horse which could be useful as both artillery horse and a heavy cart-horse for peace-time work. The history of the country had a certain influence on the breed. Schleswig Province belonged at one time to Denmark, and since that time one may often find a dash of blood of heavy Danish horse in the Schleswig horse.

In the latter half of the last century when the demand for horses of every description, and for every purpose, was great indeed, the Schleswig horse was not unknown in England. When satisfying the needs of the farmer and tradesman the horse-dealer was always catholic in his tastes and, if any breed was available and likely to carry out the work required of it with reasonable satis-faction, a place was found for it on the market. Hence there was a considerable flow of horses, Schleswigs and many other breeds constantly being imported, chiefly from Holland, Germany, Belgium and France. The dealer was always sensible to the virtues of many of the Continental breeds.

As the smallest of all breeds of ponies, the Shetland is known throughout the whole of the civilised world, and is remarkable for being probably the strongest member of the equine world in relation to its size. The pony's origin is unknown, but records of its existence in the Shetland Isles, lying to the north of Scotland, date back many centuries. Its diminutive size is thought to be due to the severe climate of the regions where it lives, but this is not entirely true, as generations of specimens bred in the South of England and elsewhere seem to increase little if anything in size. In the islands the pony certainly has much to endure, especially at the end of a severe winter and before the spring grass appears, and often has to rely on seaweed for its food.

Not until the middle of the 19th century was any attempt made in the way of selective breeding, and it was a few years prior to this that the pony was first used in the coal pits. Previously to that, its general use in the islands was, in spite of its size, as a saddle-pony and as a pack-pony, generally for carting seaweed for fertilising the ground. The great demand from the pits caused the breeding of these ponies to flourish, and as the buyers took the best the stock became very poor in quality, until Lord Londonderry established a stud in 1870 in the Islands of Bressay and Noss. His stallion " Jack " as a foundation sire became famous and has had a profound influence on the breed.

Owing to the growing number of mines which are now electrified, the demand for the pony has decreased in recent years and it has become increasingly evident that the pony's market is more that of a saddle-pony for children, for whom, owing to its docile and tractable character, it is well suited. Added to this, it has a picturesque and quaint beauty quite unlike any other breed. Withal, it is a lovable character and is deservedly popular, and much kept just as a pet. Although practically never seen in harness in England there is a considerable export of Shetlands for this purpose to Holland and the U.S.A.

Description. Small, refined and short head carried high, with neat short ears. Muzzle small with pronounced nostrils, and large kindly eye. Relatively long and strong neck, meeting the head with a small gullet. The short, strong back must be deep through the girth with well-sprung ribs and sloping shoulders and pronounced withers. Strong and long in quarters with tail set high and carried gaily, limbs must be markedly strong with long forearms and thighs, large knees and hocks with flat bone below and very short in the cannon bone. The feet are relatively small but round and open. The coat is fine and thick, giving great protection. The summer coat is sleek and fine. Abundant mane, tail and forelock with little hair on the heels, and all lacking in curl. Action straight and true, light and airy. *Size* : Limited by the Stud Book to 10·2 hands, but average about 9·3 ; a pony considerably smaller has a great " pet " market. *Colour*, black, brown and bay followed by grey, dun and chestnut. Piebalds and skewbalds are found. *General characteristics* : Long-lived and breed to an old age ; extraordinary strength for size ; great hardiness with ability to thrive on poorest soil ; almost complete freedom from disease ; surefooted and easily handled.

In order to produce a pony for the coal-mines somewhat smaller than the Dartmoor, a number of farmers and others have, for a number of years past, run Shetland stallions with Dartmoor mares and these are allowed to roam the moors more or less in a wild state. To those farmers who are jealous of the purity of the Dartmoor breed, this has caused great distress, and strenuous efforts have been made to put an end to this evil, apparently, though, with little or no success. No one would wish to curtail ordered cross-breeding on any lines, but the indiscriminate casting loose of one breed with another where no control is possible is to be condemned.

BREED SOCIETY : The Shetland Pony Stud Book Society.

Both in height and weight the Shire horse is the greatest of England's agricultural horses and was used to a considerable extent in all large towns throughout the country. Its origin may be traced to a breed of heavy horse which was certainly in existence in Elizabethan times and was referred to by historians of those days as the Great Horse of England. That a horse of bulk and great strength was required in those days is certain, when it is remembered that the war horse was needed to carry men in armour weighing perhaps 30 stone. He had also to draw heavy, rough, springless carts over tracks, which is the best that can be said of the so-called roads of those days, or over country where roads did not exist. This, then, was the forbear of the Shire Horse, which some 200 years ago came to be known by that name.

In England the horse is bred largely in the deep and heavy-soiled counties of Lincoln, Cambridge and Huntingdon, where his enormous strength makes him popular as an agricultural horse. The best of the breed stand over 17 hands and are capable of pulling a net weight of 5 tons, and although perhaps the slowest worker of the heavy breeds, the Shire is a steady, level mover of great honesty.

Bays and browns are the predominating colours, while blacks and greys are less frequent, and all Shires have a considerable amount of white on the feet and legs.

In character this great horse is of a docile nature, and at three years old it can be worked on the farms, soon becoming a commercial proposition. Representatives of the breed are to be found at most horse shows where agricultural classes are to be seen.

Description. Colour, predominating colours bays and browns, then blacks and greys. *Height*, 16·2 to 17·3 hands ; average about 17 hands. *Head*, lean in proportion to body, neither too large nor too small. *Forehead*, broad between the eyes. *Eyes*, large, prominent and docile in appearance. *Nose*, nostrils thin and wide, lips together and nose slightly roman. *Ears*, long, lean, sharp and sensitive. *Throat*, clean-cut and lean. *Shoulders*, deep and oblique and wide enough for the collar to rest on. *Neck*, fairly long, slightly arched, well set up to give the horse a commanding appearance.

BREED SOCIETY : The Shire Horse Society.

SPANISH

Before the Saracens invaded Spain and brought
with them a large number of Barb and Arab
horses, which in consequence greatly improved
the native stock, a Spanish horse was a big-headed
animal and heavy in the barrel, although with good
feet and legs. The crossing of that Spanish horse
with Barbs and Arabs resulted in the Spanish
Jennet, famous for its beauty, great docility and
obedience. Their main characteristics were a
great width of breast, powerful shoulders, roman
noses, long arched neck with full and flowing
mane, goose rumps, and rather extravagant high
action so much appreciated later on in the Vienna
" High School," where they excelled at the
" Spanish Walk."

This proud, showy action and splendid appearance recommended them for studs in Austria and

Italy, where special breeds were created such as Kladruber, Lippizana and the Neapolitan horse, which was used for parades.

The Spanish Jennet described by Berenger as " docile and affectionate to man yet full of spirit and courage " deserved the highest praise from the Duke of Newcastle in " A New Method of Dress Horses " :

. . . if well-chosen, is the noblest horse in the world . . . the most beautiful that can be, for he is not so thin and lady-like as the Barb, nor so gross as the Neapolitan. He is of great spirit and of great courage and docile, hath the proudest walk, the proudest trot and the best action in his trot ; the loftiest gallop, the swiftest careers and is the lovingest and gentlest horse and fittest of all for a King in day of Triumph . . . much more intelligent than even the best Italian horses, and for that reason the easiest dressed, because they observe too much with their eyes, and their memories are too good.

They made " absolutely the best stallions in the world to breed horses for War, Manège, Ambling pad-horses, and for running horses."

The best Spanish Jennets were bred in the Spanish Royal Stud at Cordova and are supposed to descend from the Barb stallion called " The Cusman " and Andalusian mares.

Later, the Spanish horses degenerated considerably, except the Andalusian breed, which goes back to the Middle Ages and carries much Arabian and Barb blood, and which in the past provided a large proportion of army remounts. Today the most important stud in Spain is at Jerez, where are bred " warm-blood " horses.

SPITI and BHUTIA

Anyone who has travelled in Kashmir, Ladakh or towards the borders of Nepal will be familiar with the sight of long strings of pack-ponies plodding patiently and securely under huge loads up and down the narrow, dizzy paths of the Himalaya, with the characteristic short, quick step, head down and apparently half asleep, but always on the alert to nip somebody or something. He will probably have used them himself for carrying his own kit and will have ridden them— and once you have ridden a hill pony of the Himalaya you do not easily forget it, especially that terrifying habit they all have of keeping always to the extreme edge of a mountain path, so that one leg dangles over several hundred feet of nothingness. The reason for this is, of course, the fact that the animal is used to carrying a wide pack on either side of his body, so he keeps to the outside of a track to avoid bumping against the cliff wall on the inner side.

The general characteristics of the hill pony, whose origin is certainly Mongolian, are the same all over the Himalaya and the highlands of Central Asia, but there are two characteristic breeds in India, the Spiti and the Bhutia, which it is convenient to deal with together   The former takes its name from the Spiti tract, a very mountainous region which lies in the Kangra District between Kulu, where the apples come from, and the central spine of the Himalaya. The breeding of these animals is one of the main sources of income of the inhabitants, who do a good trade in them with the surrounding hill districts and states, extending even into Tibet. The breeding is mainly in the hands of one tribe, Kanyats, who are high caste

Hindus, and is carried out in small units of two or three, and never more than six mares. The Kanyats are very proud of their hereditary calling, and claim to be able to distinguish representatives of this breed in any unknown drove of ordinary hill ponies.

Mares usually have their first foal at four years, and March and April are the foaling months. Very little attention is paid to the care of mares and foals, and they live on what they can pick up on the mountainsides. Inbreeding is practised to keep down the size, and breeding is usually from parent to progeny rather than from brother to sister.

The Spiti is small, tough, thickset, up to plenty of weight and very surefooted. It has an intelligent head with remarkably sharp ears, strong, short back, short legs with good bone, and hard round feet. The neck is short and thick, tapering slightly towards the head; the shoulders are sturdy and straightish, the ribs well sprung and quarters well developed. It thrives only in the cold heights of the Himalaya, and in spite of its hard life it is full of character and humour, and is tireless and apparently indestructible.

The Bhutia pony is bred in parts of Nepal and other Himalayan regions from the Punjab to Darjeeling. It has much the same characteristics as the Spiti, except that it is slightly bigger, averaging 13 to 13·2 hands as against the 12 hands of the latter. The predominant colours of both breeds are grey and iron grey.

STANDARD BRED

This is the official name of the famous American trotting and pacing horses. Harness racing, whether trotting or pacing (which is the lateral movement as opposed to the diagonal), may be said to hold pride of place in popularity as a horse spectacle with the American public ; and these animals are bred and trained with extreme care and with truly American scientific efficiency.

The father of the modern Standard trotter was Rysdyk's " Hambletonian," also known as " Hambletonian 10 " from his Standard number in the register. Foaled in 1849 he descended in three ways (direct male line and two collateral crosses) from the English Thoroughbred " Messenger," the *fons et origo* of all American trotting horses, who, himself the son of the Norfolk

Trotter " Bellfounder," was imported to America in 1788. And through him the breed goes back in the male line, through " Blaze," to the Darley Arabian. Allied with this principal foundation element are many other Thoroughbred strains, and also Morgan, Norfolk Trotter, and other light horse strains.

The Standard Bred trotter breed dates officially from 1879, when the National Association of Trotting Horse Breeders adopted a set of rules for admission to the American Trotting Register (first published in 1871) based on speed. The rules have been varied from time to time according to the great progress made in the establishment of the type, and now the Standard, from being largely one of performance and speed on the race track, is one of blood only. Selective breeding under the Standard has transformed an initially composite type into a homogeneous and firmly established one, renowned the world over ; and the trotting horses of Europe all owe something to the American breed.

The characteristics of the breed are generally Thoroughbred, with modifications due to differences in gait and work. In the main the Standard Bred is heavier-limbed and more robustly built than the Thoroughbred, with longer body, shorter legs and greater endurance. The average height is 15·2 hands ; 16 hands is seldom reached, while 15 hands is usually the lower limit. The weight in racing condition is 900 to 1,000 lb. The horse possesses unequalled heart and stamina, which enable it to run heat after heat at top speed without flagging.

BREED SOCIETY : The United States Trotting Association.

STRELETS

The study of the breeds of Russian horses compared with those of most continental countries, particularly Germany and Austria, emphasises the fact that so many breeds of these owe their existence, and certainly their development, to the individual effort. Many well-known breeds have been " made " at certain large studs and indeed have taken the name of the stud as their breedname. Examples of this can be found of course in other parts of the world. In Britain, however, the naming of breeds is entirely territorial, if we except the Percheron (q.v.), which, though firmly established there, is of French breeding. The Russian Strelets is an instance of stud-naming.

This horse is numbered among the more aristocratic of the Russian breeds of horses and might fairly be called with truth the Russian Arab. The source from which this good breed was built was in native mares from that mountainous regions of the Ukraine; these were the foundation stock of the stud, and the selected of them were then crossed with Anglo-Arab, Turkish, Persian or pure Arab sires. The progeny of these —the Strelets—are now breeding true to type. This breed can be described as a large Arab, with all the excellent attributes of that ancient race, and is unaffected apparently in spite of being bred for greater size. It is much admired as a supreme riding horse and is particularly valuable for cavalry needs and therefore in much demand.

SUFFOLK

One outstanding characteristic of the Suffolk
Horse, which is also known as the Suffolk Punch,
is that it is *always* chestnut in colour. No other
colour is seen, and if it were, would not be
tolerated. Furthermore, it shares distinctiveness
with the British Percheron of being the only clean-
legged British draught horse. It is indigenous
to the County of Suffolk on the eastern side
of England, and, according to Camden's " Brit-
tannia," the Suffolk Horse dates back to 1506.
A curious feature in connection with this breed
is that every specimen of the breed now in existence traces its descent in direct male line in an
unbroken chain to a horse foaled in 1760.

It is unnecessary to point out that the Suffolk

has varied since those early days by the infusion of blood from certain strains possessed of a finer forehand, greater activity and perhaps a more elegant conformation. All this has produced what is now a very handsome horse with a fine record of performance, for the Suffolk will work well as a two-year-old and go on until it is in the mid-twenties, and withal it is a very economical horse to keep, doing well on little and poor feed at that. It should be mentioned that, with rare exceptions, it is very docile.

In height it stands about 16 hands, and, unlike the Clydesdale, it should have great width in front and in the quarters. Another feature of the horse is its short legs and consequent low draught, giving great direct pull on its vehicle. Its great body is a feature, and the horse is possessed of a round and friendly yet impressive appearance which is very marked. The fact that it can, if asked, trot in a way which can hardly be expected of the Shires and Clydesdales, is claimed in its favour. Old records in the form of advertisements show that many matches were held in weight-carrying contests in the County of Suffolk, which would seem to show that the pulling potentialities of the Suffolk, even in those days, was well recognised.

Much has been said and written in years past of the supposed unsoundness of the feet of the Suffolk, and it is generally accepted that there was then real foundation for this. It can be stated, however, that it is many years since breeders have had to consider this real defect, and the Suffolk is now a sound-footed animal.

Description. Colour, chestnut, a star or a little white on face is no detriment. *Head*, big, with broad forehead. *Neck*, deep in collar, tapering gracefully towards the setting of the head. *Shoulders*, long and muscular, well-thrown back at wither. *Body*, deep, round ribbed from shoulder to flank, with graceful outline in back, loin and hind-quarters; wide in front and behind; the tail well up with good second thighs. *Feet, joints and legs*, the legs should be straight with fair sloping pasterns, big knees and long clean hocks on short cannon-bones free from coarse hair. Elbows turned in regarded as a serious defect. Feet having plenty of size with circular form protecting the frog. *Walk and trot*, smart and true, with well-balanced and good action.

With so admirable a foundation it is not surprising that efforts have been made by many to cross the Suffolk with Thoroughbreds and Arabs in the endeavour to evolve heavy-weight hunters and cobs. These attempts in general have met with varying success, as must always be the case where violent admixture of hot and cold blood is used as a first cross. None the less many good specimens have been produced which have from time to time evoked great enthusiasm. Cross-breeding of this nature, however, must always carry with it an abnormal degree of chance.

BREED SOCIETY : The Suffolk Horse Society.

Besides the native pony type already described (see Scandinavian) there is in Sweden a general utility type of horse, the result of crosses between the local " cold-blooded " horses of the north and west of Europe and the " warm-blooded " animals from the East, the latter blood not direct but through various European breeds. These in recent times have been mainly Anglo-Norman and Hanoverian stallions, which have introduced Thoroughbred strains into the native stock and brought about a considerable improvement in the breed.

The resulting type is a compromise between ride and draught, the army demanding remounts more and more Thoroughbred in character and agriculture requiring heavier and stronger animals for farm work. In general this type is a "warm-blooded" horse, strong, compact, with short clean legs and a good temperament, useful for both saddle and draught.

In Northern Sweden there is a special type of draught horse, known as the North Swedish Horse. Earlier attempts to establish the breed had failed, but in 1900 an association was formed with the object of creating the North Swedish Horse. The method was a steady grading-up of the existing local stock by crosses to Gudbrandsdals from Norway (see Scandinavian), and proved successful. In 1944 there were 400 stallions in service to about 15,000 mares a year, producing some 8,000 pure North Swedish horses annually. By then the importation of Gudbrandsdal had practically stopped, but the Oldenburg (*q.v.*) was being imported in increasing numbers.

The North Swedish Horse is eminently suited to light-draught agricultural work in Northern Sweden.

The most popular heavy-draught horse in Sweden is the Swedish Ardennes, comprising more than 60 per cent. of the country's horse stock. The Ardennes (*q.v.*) were first introduced from Belgium in 1837 before they had been crossed with the heavier Brabançon. In 1901 a Stud Book was opened for the breed, and since 1924 the Breeding Association for the Swedish Ardennes Horse has kept pedigrees and registered all foals.

In 1950 a horse census in Sweden showed the number of horses of all ages to be 439,760. Of these about 16,000 were "warm-blood" horses, 138,000 "cold-blood" light-draught, and 286,000 "cold-blood" heavy-draught.

TARBENIAN

The cradle of this famous breed is the country in the neighbourhood of the small, quiet town of Tarbes, at the foot of the Pyrenees, by the River Adour. The origin of the breed must be searched for in the Iberian horse, which at the beginning of the 19th century was improved by Arabian stallions imported by Napoleon Bonaparte. During his rule a great many excellent Arab stallions came to France. After his fall and during the so-called Restoration of the monarchy, Bourbons imported English Thoroughbred stallions, which augmented the height of the Tarbenian horse, and thus was created the Bigourdan horse. Later (1833–1852) the Administration de Harras in Tarbes made certain efforts to improve the Anglo-Arab for general service, and in the result the " Bigourdan amelioré " (improved Bigourdan) was created. This horse was quite fixed in type until the end of the 19th century, having been submitted to the permanent contribution of the Arab horse as well as of the English Thoroughbred.

In the opinion of the French connoisseurs, the introduction of English Thoroughbred blood, without any limits or control, during the Restoration had a rather disastrous influence on the type of the Tarbenian horse, so there was later a tendency to add more Arabian blood. It is interesting to quote the theory of A. E. Pease concerning this breed in his work " Horse Breeding " :

The foundation of this breed is from Navarre blood, and the Navarian breed owes its origin to the Andalusian. He, however, degenerated in France to the type known as "Cheval Navarrin" the Horse of Navarra, and became a light, weedy animal, slack backed, heavy shouldered, and having little of Andalusian except in a thick heavy neck. He retained, however, high graceful action and an elegance and suppleness that made him an agreeable hack. The problem was to add strength and size without depriving the breed of its quality, grace and action. First, recourse was had to English Thoroughbred blood alone, but this was abandoned, and the mares were sent first to English blood, and their produce being mares, to Arab blood and the produce of this cross to English blood again, giving a most successful result. In the last years of the 19th century, the Bigourdan, having the contour fixed and the height increased, was no longer merely a light saddle horse, but was adapted for light carriages also.

What is the Tarbenian horse today ? Nothing else but Anglo-Arab bred for more than a century in the plain which surrounds Tarbes. As the animal, as well as man, submits to the influence of soil and climate, so does the Tarbenian horse. If not refreshed by English and Arabian imports it becomes very similar to the local horse which existed before the Tarbenian breed was established. This circumstance requires the permanent infusion of English Thoroughbred and Arabian blood.

The Tarbenian horse is a light-boned horse standing about 15 hands, of good conformation and having beautiful action. Common colours are dark brown and chestnut, seldom grey. His qualities, endurance, speed, great courage, unexacting food requirements and very great intelligence make him an excellent horse for cavalry as well as for sporting purposes. The general opinion of experts is that in this breed one may easily pick up 80 horses out of 100 that are very good ones for the above-mentioned purposes.

TENNESSEE WALKING HORSE

Although the official name of this horse is the Tennessee, it is better and more popularly known in America as the Plantation Walking Horse, which indicates the special purpose for which it was produced, to carry the farmers and planters of the South at a comfortable pace over their plantations. Like the Morgan Horse (*q.v.*), this breed owes its foundation to one powerful pre-potent stallion (known as " Black Allan," from his colour) a Standard Bred trotting stallion of mixed Hambletonian and Morgan ancestry. Foaled in 1886, he was taken to Tennessee as a colt, and like " Justin Morgan," the progenitor of the Morgan breed, had a long life at stud and produced numerous progeny, mainly from the Tennessee mares of mixed Thoroughbred, pacing and saddle-horse strains. He was a sire of great prepotency, reproducing his type regularly and carrying on the blood with all its power in succeeding generations with constant uniformity. The breed was a natural production from the needs of the place and times, and established itself as a most popular and useful type purely on its own merits.

The Walking Horse is a much heavier and more powerful animal than the American Saddle Horse (q.v.), and is generally larger, stouter, more robust and less elegant than the latter. The head is large and plain, neck rather short, body and quarters solid and massive, with heavier limbs. The prevailing colours are bay, black and chestnut, while roan is common and greys are also found. He is temperate by disposition, intelligent and well-mannered. His principal characteristic, from which he derives his name, Walking Horse, is the running walk, fast, easy and enduring, the gait which is so much favoured by the Southern planters and farmers. Careful training is needed to develop the true running gait, which is liable to turn into the pace if pressed.

In addition, he also has other paces : a good ordinary walk ; he canters well ; and is a good trotter in harness. Members of this breed have for a long time been widely used for agricultural work on farms, as well as for riding, and are undoubtedly first-class general-purpose animals, useful on the farm, between the shafts, or under saddle. In weight he runs to 1,000 lb. and over, and in height is seldom below 15·2 hands.

BREED SOCIETY : The Tennessee Walking Horse Breeders' Association of America.

THOROUGHBRED (English)

The name is synonymous with the present-day racehorse, and the Thoroughbred is the best-known of all British breeds, famous throughout the world, and to a large extent represents all that is best in the horse world; indeed the Thoroughbred sets a degree of excellence in points which has become a standard. It should, however, be borne in mind that the English Thoroughbred is, in fact, of foreign blood, and Lady Wentworth writes in " Horses of Britain " :

The English Thoroughbred, though foreign by blood, is called " English " because of the long time it has been bred and developed in England, and " Thoroughbred " because it originated from the Arabic " Kehilan " of which " Thoroughbred " is the literal translation, and which is the generic term for the Arabian breed, meaning pure-bred all through.

All Thoroughbreds trace their ancestry to three Arabian sires, and their names are well known—the Darley Arabian, the Godolphin Arabian and the Byerley Turk. Much has been written to suggest that these famous horses were put to English mares, but there can, in fact, be no question that the foundation mares were Eastern mares and no doubt Arabian. As time went on, less and still less Arab blood was introduced, and the desire for more speed became paramount and more insistent, for today the Arab cannot live with the Thoroughbred in any test of speed, for the latter has become truly a racing machine, and a very wonderful one at that. Even now times tend to become even faster and with it the prices of such stock become more spectacular.

The value of the breed, therefore, being based almost entirely on speed, those which cannot win on the racecourse, unless possessed of some admixture in their breeding which is particularly sought after, tend to become of little value. The great majority of the horses are gelded, and they and the mares find a market among those seeking hunters, hacks and even polo ponies. Latterly the market for unwanted Thoroughbred mares has become somewhat more " open " to cross with the Arab, producing as they do a most desirable animal in the Anglo-Arab (*q.v.*), often an animal of exceptional beauty, with a more equable temperament than the Thoroughbred. The Thoroughbred is much used as a sire to produce hunters.

The Thoroughbred at its best is a very beautiful horse, perhaps the most beautiful in the world, with the exception of the Arab. It must be stated, however, that as the result of a number of contributory causes, much unsoundness in wind and limb exists.

A *description* of the horse must be that of the highest class of light horse in existence. The head refined, the neck elegant and arched, withers pronounced, and the shoulder very sloping ; legs, clean, hard and of good bone with tendons pronounced. The back short, the body deep with ribs well-sprung to barrel shape, the croup high. Tail well set and quarters generous to a degree with hocks well let down, standing true and moving with a great striding action. The whole, one of intense refinement and indicative of great speed.

The position of the Thoroughbred in the world of horses is an enviable one for two very potent reasons. Flat-racing and steeplechasing are so firmly established, constituting now almost a national industry, that it seems inconceivable that any elimination or marked reduction in the sport need be feared. No other breed of horse can ever take the place of the Thoroughbred on account of its speed, even if any other breed were made eligible for entry at Weatherby and Sons, which again is inconceivable. The breed stands unchallenged as a racehorse.

The preceding pages have shown repeatedly that the Thoroughbred, along with the Arab, is the main source of up-grading of very many breeds. As this has been practised for centuries it may be fairly assumed that its value is proved beyond possibility of doubt.

The Jockey Club is the body controlling flat-racing in England.

TIMOR PONY

This pony is of good repute in Australia and New Zealand, and has always been well used in harness and under saddle. It is also to be seen at times in the show ring. Although permitted colours are not defined—indeed it seems the breed is found in any colour—it is interesting that such an attractive admixture frequently occurs as chocolate body, cream spots and cream mane and tail, suggesting the Appaloosa type. The illustration, of a six-months-old filly, indicates a well-bodied pony of good girth, strong across the back and quarters.

These Timor ponies are eager, sure-footed and tireless, and possessed of considerable natural wisdom. Because of this they are largely used for stock work, for which they are admirably suited, since quite heavy weights seem to trouble them not at all.

Undoubtedly the best German breed is the East Prussian horse. East Prussia, the biggest horse-breeding centre of the German Reich before the end of the Second World War, used to supply to the German Army the largest number of remounts, while before the war breeding East Prussian foals and selling them as yearlings was an extremely profitable proposition for local farmers.

The most prominent role in the foundation of the East Prussian breed was played by the Trakehnen Stud, founded in 1732 by William I of Prussia (father of Frederick the Great), who supplied both the land and the foundation breeding material, partly from Royal Studs and partly by importation of many high-class Arabs from

Prince Radziwill's Stud at Taurogi, in Poland. Trakehnen horses soon became the pride of German horse-breeding, and Trakehnen Stud became the *pépinière* of the East Prussian breed.

The Trakehnen Stud, which has a 200-year-old tradition and more, lies in the north-western part of East Prussia and, looking at the beautifully drained plains with excellent pastures well supplied with lime and phosphorus to give horses good bone, one could hardly believe that in the first quarter of the 18th century the same place was swampy and only covered by shrubs.

The Trakehnen horse is a beautiful and good-tempered animal, well ribbed, standing about 16 hands, with strong back and having a very good action, and could surely be considered as the perfect military saddle-horse if he had more resistance and was more hardy. The horse comes of local and Smudish origin (which is next door to East Prussia) the breed graded up by Arabs and English Thoroughbreds of heavier type. Just before the Second World War, the Germans, to improve the breed, looked for a long time for a suitable high-class Arab stallion, and finally found one in Poland.

In the Trakehnen Stud the service period begins towards the end of November and foals are left with their dams until four and a half months old. As three-year-olds they go to the training establishment, which is on the spot, where they remain for a year. When they are four-year-olds they are submitted to trials which include hunting with packs of hounds and cross-country races, the obstacles being fences, banks and open ditches. The best ones are retained for breeding in Trakehnen Stud, the second best go to State studs, the third class being sold to private breeders. These three classes are branded with a stamp of Trakehnen (stag's horns) on the right shoulder, varying in different classes, while those who did not pass the test are castrated and go as remounts to the army. The important role in improvement of the Trakehnen horse was played by the stallion " Perfectionist " by " Persimmon " out of " Perfect Dream of Morion." The best offspring during the war were produced by the stallions " Persival " and " Dampfross von Dingo." The association of breeders of light horse of Trakehnen origin counted 10,000 members with 20,000 mares registered, while four State studs bred army remounts in East Prussia from 500 stallions and 33,000 mares.

From the foregoing it will be seen that this famous breed has been fostered with characteristic German thoroughness, for it is doubtful whether any organised breeding has insisted on such exhaustive training as was undertaken at the Trakehnen Stud. It is hard to imagine, too, an association watching over the interests of one breed of light horse claiming a membership of 10,000. This is a tribute to the breed, which has always been held in high esteem by horsemen of many nations. No doubt the high quality, sound constitution and stamina of the breed is largely on account of the saturation of Thoroughbred and Arab blood. The Trakehnen Stud was destroyed during the war, but the breed is extensively fostered in the southern part of East Prussia, now belonging to Poland. The identical animal is bred in large numbers in Western Germany and is known by its old name of East Prussian, which breed is identical with the Trakehnen.

TURK

But little known to the present-day student of equine history, the Turk none the less needs to be considered and its value weighed as a representative of the Eastern hot-blood family, though it must be admitted that one would be hard put to find a true Turkish horse in these days. They were undoubtedly known in England in the 16th century, and as some indication of the horse let us quote Blunderville who, in 1580, wrote of the Turk that they " be indifferent faire to the eie, though not very great nor strong made, yet verie light and swift in their running and of great courage." From this happily chosen word-picture it would appear that the horse was somewhat similar to the Barb.

As is well known, the famous " Byerley Turk "

was imported into England in 1689, though certain authorities have asserted that he was not a Turk but an Arab. The " Lister Turk " was imported by the Duke of Berwick in the reign of James II, while between the years 1690 and 1700 two horses, whose stock subsequently stamped their worth in a long line of racehorses, themselves achieved fame on the English Turf ; they were imported by Lord D'Arcy—the " White Turk " and the " Yellow Turk."

Authorities seem to agree that the old Turkoman horse was identical with the Mongolian horse of Upper Asia (see Mongolian), and if such be indeed true then it is not surprising that the Mongolian influence, despite the fact that there has been much mixing of Arab blood, asserts itself in the straight or roman nose and the ewe neck yet withal a tail fairly well set on. Such horses are to be found mainly in Anatolia.

The most typically indigenous horses in Turkey are the Kurdistan ponies bred near Sivas. There it is the custom to cross the native mares with Arab stallions, thus encouraging a general grading-up of the native breed and turning out a good type of small working pony of 14 to 14·2 hands and well suited to native requirements. The Kurdistan is of the same root stock as the Turkoman and they have coarse heads, thick necks, short bodies and good bone. As may be supposed from their breeding, they are immensely hardy and greatly enduring, while in colour they are usually grey or bay.

VIATKA

Of Klepper descent, these ponies are now regarded as a Russian breed. State pedigree studs maintain the breed's purity. They belong to the group known as the Northern Forest type, all of which are exceptionally hardy. They range from between 13 and 14 hands and are shades of bay, grey, roan or mousey dun. Somewhat long in the back, they possess strong short legs, deep chests, well-sprung ribs ; and their small heads, usually with a concave profile, are pleasantly " breedy," although the lower jaw is often massive. Some have great speed. In winter they develop an immense coat and a subcutaneous layer of fat as a protection against the extreme cold. Varieties, named after their local provinces, are Obvinkas and Kazankas, around 13 hands.

WELSH COB

Photograph by W. W. Rouch & Co., 161 Strand, London.

The virtues of the Welsh Cob are known far beyond the confines of Great Britain, for it is an animal of many virtues and of outstanding strength and activity. As a breed, too, it is old established, having its foundation in the Welsh Mountain Pony, whose antiquity really dates to a time long before any true records existed.

The Welsh Cob has had a great influence upon trotting animals in many parts of the world, and its blood has gone far in the making of the outstanding Hackney horse and pony of Great Britain. It was, too, very many years ago, used in the development of the Fell Pony, which up to comparatively recent years has been used as a trotting pony, and the records of times and distances were greatly prized in the famous Fell stallions of those days.

As may be expected, the Welsh Cob has inherited much of the hardiness of the mountain pony, which it resembles in many respects, for it should have the same small head showing a lot of quality, and the small, prick ears so characteristic of the pony. It must, too, have a strong, deeply girthed body and immensely powerful quarters with well-set-up tail, while its legs must be short and strong, standing over not too much ground and showing a broad and generous chest. In action it must be active and not show too much knee, and have with it a bold and virile carriage. Its uses are many and it can be described as the utility type. Few animals could be found more useful to the small farmer, for it is of a tractable and kindly nature and it is essentially useful for all kinds of harness work, being capable of pulling a big weight and trotting on in a way to eat up the ground.

As a riding cob its height, which may be anything from about 14 to 15·1 hands, is suitable for all sizes of riders, and a well-schooled Welsh Cob makes an ideal ride for an elderly man. At the same time it is a natural and bold jumper, and with its strength and stamina is particularly useful as a hunter, and is just the kind for a heavy and trappy country. The breeding of this useful animal is fairly general throughout Wales, but perhaps the most famous of its kind come from Cardiganshire, where the best type of Welsh Cob is to be found. A heavier cob, less of the riding type, is to be found in different parts of Wales, more particularly in the south, a horse of immense strength, which shows quite an amount of hair on the heels, very impressive, very powerful and much in demand for haulage work round the pit heads.

The true Welsh Cob is a clean-legged animal, with but a little silky hair upon its heels, having a fine mane and forelock, and its colour may be bay, brown or black, grey, roan or chestnut, and, as with the mountain pony, duns and creams are found ; but piebalds or skewbalds are not looked upon with favour, and anything in the way of a " washy " colour meets with no favour whatever,

As an indication of type hardiness and stamina it should be noted that in the pre-mechanised army days, the cob, being capable of bearing an enormous weight, was much used for military pack work and for mounted infantry. Because of this, stallions of the right type were always in demand by foreign governments for the purpose of infusing the right blood and for the production of the right type of horse for various army purposes.

In contemplating the future of the Welsh Cob of draught type and that of riding type, one can only conclude that the latter will retain its popularity in these days when any good riding horse is in such demand. It is interesting to reflect and to record the fact that in the Cob and the Mountain Pony the Welsh have two quite outstanding examples of horse-flesh.

BREED SOCIETY : The Welsh Pony and Cob Society.

WELSH MOUNTAIN

One of the most popular and by most people thought to be the most beautiful of Britain's mountain and moorland ponies, the Welsh Mountain Pony claims an existence so remote as to be incalculable. It is truly indigenous to the soil it has so long graced and on which it has thrived so well, in spite of the great hardships it has endured with the passing of the seasons. Today it is still there, on the Welsh mountains and wastes, wild or semi-wild, but always a potential joy to a riding child or to the small tradesman as an honest little worker between the shafts. The very nature of its ancestry and up-bringing gives it those priceless qualities of intelligence, pluck, soundness and endurance for which it is so justly famed.

The Welsh Mountain Pony, though so small in height, performs really remarkable feats of strength and endurance, for it carries full-grown men without any apparent effort and certainly with no ill-effects. As a children's riding-pony it is very prominent, very popular and in the show-ring is most successful. The classic beauty of its head and the gay carriage of its tail, coupled with the generous centre-piece and quarters, giving it an advantage over most other breeds.

It is claimed for the breed that the native pony mares of Wales had much to do with the breeding, in the very early days of the English Thorough-bred. It is at least certain, however, that the pony was much used for producing the polo pony, the Hackney and the Hunter, and by no means the least important, the hardy, active and gay Welsh Cob.

The Welsh Mountain Pony (not to be confused with the Welsh Pony, which is a larger animal) has a small, neat, intelligent, Arab-like head with small, prick ears and exceptionally big and thoughtful eyes, and these must be set wide apart. The line of the face is slightly dished, as in the Arab, with the muzzle fine and tapering and very soft to the touch. The neck is of good length, graceful and supple and has a natural carriage. The shoulders are deep and well-laid, and although the withers are not very pronounced, they can be relied on to take a riding saddle reasonably well. The back is markedly strong and short with good loins and tail set high and carried proudly. The limbs are short and well formed of good flat bone with hard, smooth, small feet.

Greys, browns and chestnuts predominate,

although any colour with the exception of piebalds and skewbalds is allowed. Blacks and roans, too, are found with duns and creams, the latter at times with blue or china eyes. The official regulation in regard to height is that ponies must not exceed 12 hands.

The ponies are to be found fairly well scattered throughout the less populated parts of Wales. Owing to their small stature, they have in the past been in great demand in the coal-mines, but with the growing increase in mechanisation, the demand is more now for children's riding-ponies and by the small tradesman as trappers.

For some while past there has been in children's riding classes in the British Isles keen competition between the pony of Thoroughbred type, the Welsh Mountain Pony, and latterly in competition with the part-bred Arab. The right specimen, from whichever breed or cross, makes an ideal pony for children and it is not easy to see which should stand highest in the horseman's estimation. One thing is certain and that is that the Welsh Mountain Pony on account of its beauty and temperament can hold its own with any pony of whatever breed in children's riding classes. A curious fact emerges in the showing of Welsh Mountain Ponies in the in-hand breeding classes, and it is that while the mare is usually shown as a riding-pony—that is, her long, level paces are rated highly—the stallion is produced to show as much knee and hock action as possible. In short, he is produced to resemble a hackney in movement. This is a curious anomaly and not helpful.

BREED SOCIETY : The Welsh Pony and Cob Society.

Thousands upon thousands of years ago—no one knows exactly when—prehistoric artists drew pictures on the walls of caves, pictures of animals they saw in their daily lives, and most likely hunted. Some of these ancient studies were preserved, and came to light in the 19th century in Spain and France, and thus are able to tell us across the ages what some of the creatures of those days were like. Among the animals most faithfully reproduced there was a small, pony-like creature with a large, heavy head, rather roman-nosed, and a tufted tail. Apparently the same type roams today the highlands of Central Asia.

In 1881 the skin and skull of one of these animals was obtained by the Russian explorer Colonel N. M. Przevalski, in whose honour it was named *Equus przevalskii*. It was described by Lydekker in " The Horse and its Relatives " as:

. . . being intermediate in characters between the horse on the one hand and the kiang and onager on the other, having chestnuts on all four limbs. The general colour was described as dun, with a yellowish tinge on the back, becoming lighter toward the flanks and almost white on the belly, with no dark dorsal stripe. The short and upright mane, which was not continued forward as a forelock, was dark brown, and the long coat was wavy on the head. The skull and hoofs were stated to be horse-like.

In 1902 Carl Hagenbeck of Hamburg, of menagerie fame, sent out an expedition to the Gobi to collect living specimens of this wild horse. Adults were unobtainable, but with the aid of a small army of Kirghiz Hagenbeck's agents were able to capture 32 foals. From among these, two colts eventually found their way to the London Zoological Gardens.

Since then this creature has been closely observed and studied, and naturalists generally agree that it is a distinct species and that it has affinity with the various types of prehistoric European horses whose remains have been found at Solutré and other places and whose portraits were made on the walls of the caves of Santander, La Madeleine and elsewhere.

In appearance this interesting animal is definitely horse-like, although it has asinine characteristics as well. It is about 12 hands in height, has a massive head with small ears and eyes, heavy jaws and unusually big teeth. It has a stocky, rather ungainly body, with heavy neck and straight shoulders. The tail is tufted, but not in the same way as the ass's ; the hairs at its root are much larger than those of the body and rather harsh, merging gradually into the terminal tuft. Legs are fairly slender, pasterns well sloped, hoofs definitely equine. In colour it is dun, with a mealy muzzle, a stripe, black or brown and often very faint, on the back, and some black below the knees and hocks. In summer the mane forms an erect crest, but in the winter, when the coat is long and thick, the mane to some extent falls over on the neck.

Originally discovered in the Kobdo district of Mongolia, north of the Altai Mountains, it moves about in small herds in Western Mongolia, and is very wild indeed and practically unapproachable by man. It interbreeds freely, however, with the local Mongolian ponies which roam those regions in a practically feral state.

Little need be added to this, but attention must be drawn to the influence which the Wild Horse has had, not only with the local Mongolian ponies as is shown : its type and characteristics are traceable in varying degree among the ponies of China and Burma and the breeds and types found in the northern parts of India. In addition, and as has been shown elsewhere, many of the North European breeds either trace their descent or have been influenced by Przevalski's horse. Specimens of the true Wild Horse are to be found in different parts of the world, including the Zoological Gardens at Whipsnade Park, where a stallion, born in Regent's Park in 1931, and a female, given by the Duke of Bedford in 1942, are kept, and anyone who is interested in the horse breeds of the world is advised to see these inter-interesting specimens. There are now several running in paddocks at Whipsnade.

YORKSHIRE COACH

This most useful breed is very little seen nowadays, but originated in that part of Yorkshire which is known as the East Riding. For a great number of years it was looked upon as and was indistinguishable from the Cleveland Bay, but it may be safely said that for at least 150 years it has had a separate identity.

Going back, then, perhaps to 1790 and for a number of years following that date, the Yorkshire Coach Horse emerged, and the reasons for its foundation were the enormous demands for a bigger, lighter and a more flashy type of horse for the more elegant vehicles which were appearing in fashionable London. For this purpose the basis was the Thoroughbred used with the Cleveland Bay. Records show that the original Thoroughbred sires used for the purpose were " Neck-romancer " (1816) and " Servetur," by " High Flyer " out of a " Matchem " mare. Certainly the names of these horses appeared in the pedigrees of well-known early Yorkshire Coach Horses of the period, " Ebor," " Paulinus " and " Seberus," while other Thoroughbred sires associated in the early days of the breed were " Goliath " and " Harpham Turk." But the breeders of those days were not content only with this cross, but used at varying times an infusion of Eastern blood, Arabs and Barbs, and these were used much on Yorkshire cart mares.

Such being the foundations of this breed, it will be seen readily that there were great variations in size and type, and it was only with the passing of very many years that anything like a fixed type became evident. Moreover, throughout that period and through the middle and latter half of the past century, which was the heyday of the carriage horse in London and the big provincial cities and, indeed, throughout the length and breadth of the land, this horse was rightly in great demand and of high reputation. The county of Yorkshire has always been famous for horse-breeding, and the fixed type of Yorkshire Coach Horse and the breeding of hunters enhanced its reputation.

The horse may be described as big and powerful, and still showing its Cleveland Bay ancestry. It is an impressive animal both in regard to substance and height, which may be up to 16·2 hands. The body is long on comparatively short legs, giving it the general appearance of being close to the ground. The girth is deep and, as befits a horse bred entirely for road work, it must have sound feet and somewhat broad. Again, as the Yorkshire Coach Horse is an animal for draught purposes the chest is broad, strong and impressive, with the shoulders heavy and muscular, so necessary for that class of work. There must be every indication of muscle over all, giving the general appearance of undoubted power.

Unhappily, this very fine old breed is hard to find, for there is little place for him in the horse world of today. Post-war coaches have been largely horsed by nondescript teams, teams from the Continent, and Hackneys, or indeed by the Yorkshire's ancestor, the Cleveland Bay. This is an unhappy thought for lovers of a good horse, for that is undoubtedly what the Yorkshire Coach Horse is.

BREED SOCIETY : The Yorkshire Coach Horse Society.

The term " Zebra," a word of Amharic origin meaning " striped," is not the title of a breed of the horse family but the descriptive name given to the three distinct species of *Equus*, all three entirely unrelated, which have retained the stripes which are said to have been a past characteristic of other members of the family. Vestiges of which remain in duns, certain primitive pony breeds and in some of the wild ass species, e.g. the onager and the kiang.

From time immemorial, unlike their cousin the horse (*Equus caballus*), the Zebras have inhabited Africa and nowhere else, being found up and down the continent from Abyssinia to the Cape, exclusive of the North African coast. There are a number of local varieties named after their discoverers, Burchell, Hartman, Grant, and so on, but they are all members of one or other of three separate species : Grevy's Zebra, the Mountain Zebra and the Quagga.

Grevy's Zebra, which is the one illustrated here, is the largest of the striped horses, averaging about 13 hands. Its chief distinguishing marks are long, expanded, and round-tipped ears, very small warts, and the pattern of its stripes, which are very regular and uniform in size, with an almost right-angle change from vertical to horizontal at the head and quarters. The stripes on the neck are broader than those on the body. The longitudinal spinal stripe broadens out considerably on the croup. Its donkey-like bray is also a distinctive characteristic. It lives on the open, scrub-covered plains in the lowlands of Abyssinia, Somaliland and northern Kenya.

The Mountain Zebra has its habitat in the mountains of the Cape provinces, Bechuanaland and what was German South-west Africa. It differs from Grevy's Zebra in having more pointed and ass-like ears, slightly more breedy looking head and in the presence of a dew-lap on the throat. The stripes are much the same, except that those on the quarters are very broad, and curve more gradually from vertical on the flanks to horizontal on the quarters and thighs. This animal is the smallest of the three species, averaging about 10 hands. It appears to be quite silent, as far as anyone can tell. The late R. I. Pocock, F.R.S., who made a close study of it in captivity states that he never heard it utter a sound.

The Quagga as it now exists is found in East and North-east Africa, excluding Egypt, and is very like the Mountain Zebra in appearance, with even more sweeping lines of broad stripes curving from flanks to quarters. It formerly inhabited South Africa as well and was first discovered there, but for some unexplained reason south of the Zambesi it lost most of its stripes, having none on the legs and hind-quarters below the tail and only faint ones on the flanks ; but this typical race is now extinct. It received its name from its very distinctive voice, rather like the repetition of the three syllables, " qua-ha-ha," which led the Hottentots to call it the " Khoua Khoua," from which the Boers evolved " Quagga."

In general all the zebra species are very asinine in appearance, with stocky bodies, heavy heads, very thick necks, straight shoulders and box-like hoofs. Although Hayes and a few others have succeeded at various times in putting odd specimens to drive between shafts, they have never really proved amenable to domestication and training. At one time Zebras, especially the mountain species, were in grave danger of extermination, but it is good to know that these interesting and picturesque members of the horse family are now strictly protected.

It is unnecessary to say that the Zebra is a most remarkable-looking animal, but its fantastic markings are a marvellous camouflage in its natural surroundings. Fortunately Zebras are usually to be found in Zoos, where their strangeness can be contemplated to the full.

With such a vivid appearance, it is obvious the Zebra would be a good act in a circus. Unfortunately, however, the animal is unco-operative and takes most unkindly to any form of tuition. Nevertheless, and it is a great tribute to their trainers' patience and skill, these strange creatures are to be seen in circus acts.

ZEELAND HORSE

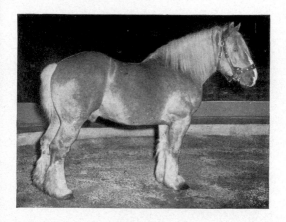

The prototype of the Zeeland horse,* a product
of the Netherlands, goes back to the earliest times,
and similar types are found in Brabant and
Limburg. In the days of the invasion by Julius
Caesar the Romans in " The Low Lands on the
Sea " came across a horse that was very strong and
massive ; speaking of these fertile lands, so rich
in pasture, the monk Drogon de Bergues Saint
Winnoq said : " There is an island, called
Walcheren, which is very rich in foodstuffs and
population, where a breed of horses is found, big-
sized and of remarkable spirit and strength."

* The name has disappeared as an official denomi-
nation according to the Netherlands Ministry of
Agriculture.

Thus the Zeeland horse became well known at a very early date, and in the Middle Ages it was used by adventurous knights in the wars they were waging, and even then was exported to England, Germany and the western parts of France.

From that time onwards these horses have been in great demand : in the Low Lands as draught-horses ; as horses of much use to the farmer in cultivating the land ; as animals that could be equally useful in the army for horse artillery. They were made use of by the Emperor Napoleon for his horse artillery during his great campaign in Russia, and during the First World War these horses were of much use in the army.

Since the beginning of this century the Zeeland Horse has been registered in a stud-book (Stud-Book for the Dutch draught-horse, The Hague), so that each one has a number of its own. Breeders give the following details of this type :

Snub-nosed head with straight-lined profile ; slightly projecting orbit ; flat forehead ; large, intelligent eyes ; short ears, pointing forward ; wide, open nostrils ; broad, deep chest ; close to the ground ; very muscular loins, flanks wide apart ; very muscular rumps and legs ; strong neck of moderate length ; plenty of bone with excellent feet and good carriage.

This combination, at first sight unwieldy, is in reality one of some elegance, and on the whole this horse differs from the Belgian by greater elegance and a more lively carriage, while, at the same time, it is bigger than the horse from the Ardennes. In this way people in Holland try to breed a horse, which, though big and heavy, is supple in its movements. It is claimed that the Zeeland Horse can bear cold and heat, possessing great adaptability under all circumstances. In character it is very suitable for work in the field, being quiet and possessed of much stamina and strength. It is a strong horse, full of spirit, yet very easy to handle.

Stallions are used for breeding from the age of three. The breeders, who are appointed by the Ministry of Agriculture, select them from the type asked for. This is a choice that is very difficult to make, and a horse that has not been selected by this Committee is not allowed to be used for breeding purposes. The foals are checked by a Stud-Book Inspector as soon as possible. He notes their characteristics and markings and the foal is registered. At the age of three the good species are ied before a Stud-Book Committee, by whom they are registered.

These horses have been used surprisingly, but with considerable success, as Liberty Horses at Bertram Mills' Circus in London, and at various circuses on the Continent. It is to be presumed that circus managements know best what appeals to their public, but the heavy horse by reason of its bulk cannot be expected to give an airy and graceful display which is the great essential of a Liberty Horse act. From the horseman's point of view, the merit of a Liberty Act by heavy horses, be they Zeeland or any other breed, lies in the fact that so much co-operation can be obtained from breeds of cold blood.

The wide grasslands of Lithuania have always been *par excellence* a fine horse-producing country, sending animals in pre-war days to most countries of Europe, including even Ireland. The country being then, as now, a Russian province, they were all comprehensively known as Russians. These, however, were not the pure native breed, which is known as the Zemaitukas and has rarely been seen in Western Europe. The name comes from "Zemaitifa," the name for the western part of Lithuania. The plural form of the word is Zemaitukai.

The Zemaitukai are of very ancient origin, and the two main ancestral strains, those which at all events have had the most influence on the primitive type, were the Tartar pony of the steppes (Przevalski or Mongolian horse) and the Arab, from animals brought by invading Teutonic Knights from Western Europe. The latter was, and still is, the predominating strain, refreshed by new Arab stock in recent years. It was mentioned as a distinct breed as far back as the 13th century, the horses being used as cavalry in that guerilla warfare at which the knights and nobles of those regions were adept, carrying their warrior riders on raids deep into Russia as far as Moscow and Novgorod. Like all primitive breeds they were renowned for their staying power, almost indestructible legs and feet, and their ability to live as it were on the smell of a grain bag.

Between the 17th and 19th centuries, when Lithuania lost her independence, the breed deteriorated, the animals being relegated more and more to farm work, to the plough and the wagon. In 1881, however, through the initiative of a Lithuanian landowner, Prince Oginski, whose descendants up to 1939 still had pure specimens of the breed in their stables, there appeared the first Stud Book of the Zemaitukai. Up to 1919, however, a good deal of cross-breeding went on to produce a heavier draught horse to cope with improved methods of agriculture, the Russians introducing animals from the Ardennes, while the Germans in the First World War carried off numbers of native ponies and crossed them with Bavarian horses. Between the two wars, when for a short period Lithuania regained her independence, strenuous and fairly successful efforts were made to build up again the original native strain at the Lithuanian State Stud Farm at Grudzai, and to breed for riding rather than for draught.

The appearance of the Zemaitukas is extremely

characteristic. The prevailing colour is dun, with light tail and mane ; mouse colour is also found and, more rarely, bay. All have a dark dorsal stripe extending to the tail. The head is small, with bright, intelligent eyes unusually widely spaced. The arched neck is short and very muscular, with a thick, wavy mane. The powerful forehand is a distinguishing mark of the breed. The legs are strong and clean, though light in bone, and the hooves hard and well-shaped. The height varies from 13 to 15 hands and the weight from 800 to 1,000 lb. In general they are compact, sturdy, well-made animals, full of latent fire and energy, and altogether worthy representatives of the ancient primitive pony type.

It is easy to see to what type the Zemaitukas belongs from this description, which must have become very familiar to the reader, for with slight variations it is so similar to what has been written of so many of the Northern European breeds : the dun colour, the dorsal or eel stripe, the short and muscular neck and the thick wavy mane. Like all Russian horses and ponies, many of which are brought up not only in a more or less wild state but subjected to great variations of temperature, the Zemaitukas is one of the toughest horses to be found and owes much of this hardiness to the law of the survival of the fittest which, if it is harsh in itself, has done much in many parts of the world to produce so many breeds of outstanding stamina.

GLOSSARY OF TECHNICAL TERMS

Many of these definitions are based on those given in "Summerhays' Encyclopaedia for Horsemen."

Aids. Signals through which the rider directs and conveys instructions to his horse. The hands, through the reins, direct and control the forehand ; the lower part of the legs and the heels collect, control and impel the hind-quarters through application behind the girth. The voice is an additional aid, whips and spurs are artificial ones.

Air. The correct bearing of a horse in its different movements and paces, being also the correct rhythm to each of these. **Artificial Airs** consist of paces other than the normal walk, trot and canter, and can be obtained from the horse only at the will of the rider and after careful schooling. (See **High School Horse.**)

Balance. When a horse carries its own weight and that of its rider in such a way that it can use and control itself to the best advantage at all paces and in all circumstances, then it has true balance.

Bang-tail. A tail with the hair squared off close to the dock or solid part of the tail. With heavy horses, "banging-up" the tail refers to tying it up.

Barrel. General description of that part of a horse's body which, roughly, is encompassed by the ribs.

Blue feet. Dark or off-black coloured feet showing a tendency to blueness.

Buck eye. A term applied to a prominent eye, usually believed to be associated with short sight.

Calf-knee. Fore-legs which, when viewed from the side and having an imaginary line drawn through them, tend to concavity below the knees. (Also known as **Back-at-the-knee** and **Buck knee.**)

Cat-hammed. Descriptive of a horse with weak hocks that stand back and away from the natural stance.

Coffin head. A coarse, ugly head in which the jowl lacks prominence.

Colt. A male horse under the age of four.

Concave (dished face). Where the line of the face tends to be slightly hollowed, e.g. the head of the Arab horse.

Conformation. General expression to denote the make-up of a horse, whether good or bad, as a whole.

Cowhocks. Hocks which are turned inwards at the points, as in a cow.

Deep through the girth. Descriptive of a horse that is well-ribbed-up with generous depth of girth behind the elbows (see **Heart room**).

Dishing. An unlevel and faulty movement of the fore-feet which, when in motion and raised from the ground, are thrown backwards and in an outer circular move-ment to the front again.

Dorsal stripe. A stripe running down the neck and along the top of the body and sometimes to the tip of the tail ; generally black, brown, or chestnut in colour, and found most often in dun horses. (Typical of horses and ponies of Scandinavian origin.) Also called a **List**.

Elk lip. A wide and somewhat loose and overhanging upper lip.

Ewe neck. Where the line of the neck from ears to wither is concave. Such horses are said to have their necks " on the wrong way." Recognised as bad conforma-tion.

Face Markings. These include : *Blaze*, a white marking almost covering the forehead between the eyes and extending down the front of the face across the whole width of the nasal bones ; *Muzzle Markings*, including both lips and extending to the nostrils ; *Star Markings*, appearing on the forehead; *Strips Markings*, extending down the face and no wider than the flat anterior surface of the nasal bones.

Feather. Hair on all four heels, of varying density and coarseness.

Fiddle-head. A large, plain, coarse and ugly-shaped head.

Filly. A female horse under the age of four.

Flat-sided. A horse is said to be flat-sided when its ribs are not rounded or " well-sprung." Also known as **slat-** or **slab-sided**.

Foal. A colt or filly up to the age of 12 months, described accordingly as colt-foal or filly-foal.

Forehand. The head, neck, shoulders, withers and fore-legs of a horse.

Frog. V-shaped horny substance in the sole of all four feet, which acts as a shock absorber.

Glass, chalk, china or wall eye. A light blue eye, having a preponderance of white.

Goose rump. Where from the highest point behind the saddle the line runs somewhat sharply downwards to the tail. Recognised as bad conformation.

Heart Room. A term of commendation indicating depth through a horse's girth, combined with a broad and open chest (" **deep through the girth** "—*q.v.*—is also used).

Height. The height of a horse is taken from the highest part of the withers in a perpendicular line to the ground. The horse is said to stand so many hands (a hand is four inches), or so many hands and so many inches, high.

High School Horse. One trained in accordance with the principles of the classical Art of Riding and able to perform one or more classical or High School airs.

Hollow Back. Where the natural concave line of the back is exaggerated and unnatural.

Jumper's Bump. A name for the protuberance at the top of the loins, a formation erroneously supposed to increase a horse's power to jump.

Limb Markings. These include : *Coronet Markings*, white hair immediately above the hoof ; *Fetlock Markings*, around and below the fetlock joint ; *Heel Markings*, from the back of the pastern to the ergot ; *Pastern Markings*, immediately below the fetlock joint, extending downwards ; *Sock Markings*, reaching about halfway up the cannon bone ; *Stocking Markings*, extending to the knee or the hock.

Mare. The female equine animal.

Mealy nose or muzzle. Of an oatmeal colour, running well up the muzzle and having no white markings, e.g. the Exmoor.

Odd-coloured. Descriptive of a coat in which there is an admixture of more than two colours tending to merge into each other at the edges of the patches, with irregular body markings.

Over at the knee. A forward bend or curve of the knees which may be the result of excessive wear, but is often a matter of conformation. It is a disfigurement which would count against a show horse.

Over-bent. A term descriptive of an exaggerated collected action with head and neck over-bent at the poll, the chin being tucked into the breast.

Over-collected. A horse is said to be over-collected when it shows too much collection, with the head position behind the vertical.

Pacer. A horse which, instead of trotting with a diagonal action, moves like a camel, near-fore and hind together, followed by off-fore and hind ; this gives a very comfortable gait for long-distance riding and is very popular in America for shows and trotting races. The action is also known as **Ambling**, the old English name for a pacer being an **Ambler**.

Parrot Mouth. A malformation of the upper jaw; the incisor teeth overhang the lower jaw and prevent proper contact between the upper and lower incisor teeth. The condition prevents a horse from grazing and may lead to digestive troubles. It is a congenital deformity, and is often called an Overshot Mouth.

Pendulous lip. Where the under lip hangs low and lifeless.

Piebald. A horse having black and white patches over the body, and perhaps mane and tail.

Pin-toes. Toes which turn inwards; horses having such never strike themselves and pin-toes are, therefore, much less serious than those that turn out (**dishing**).

Pulled Tail. One where some of the hair at the side of the dock, as well as any excessive growth on top, has been removed by pulling to give a slim and tidy effect.

Quarter Marks. Fancy patterns made by brushing the hair in parts with a wet brush in the " wrong " direction —sometimes a stencil plate is used to help form the design. Seen mostly on racehorses and show horses.

Ragged Hips. Where the points of the hips are very prominent.

Roach-back. A prominent malformed convex spinal column, also known as **hog-back**.

Roan Colour. Where there is an admixture of white hair with the body colour, lightening the general effect of the latter. Thus *blue roan* has black or brown as the body colour, *bay* or *red roan* has bay or bay-brown, and *strawberry* or *chestnut roan* has chestnut.

Roman nose. A head with a convex front, found in the cold-blooded horse races as distinct from the hot-blooded races, which tend to the concave; e.g. " roman," the Shire Horse.

Short of a rib. Where there is a marked space between the last rib and the point of the hip, and showing a sign of slackness over the loins. A condition found in horses of defective conformation, i.e., too long a back, hind-quarters standing too far back.

Shoulders. *Sloping*—running obliquely from the point of the shoulder to the withers. In theory, the more sloping the shoulder, the better the ride. *Straight*—less oblique, and should be found in harness and draught horses, where the position and set of the neck collar is important. But a show Hackney must have oblique shoulders for the up-and-out action demanded today.

Sickle hocks. Hocks which, when looked at from the side have a sickle or crescent-like appearance, and where the line from the point of the hock to the ground slopes forward.

Skewbald. A horse with similar markings to the piebald, only with colours other than black, i.e. brown, bay, chestnut and roan.

Stallion. A horse capable of reproducing the species, also known as entire—an ungelded horse.

Standing over. A term descriptive of a horse that appears to " give " at the knees. The defect is not detrimental (except in the show-ring), unless it is caused by overwork.

Tied-in below the knee. Where the measurement immediately below the knee is less than the measurement taken lower down towards the fetlock joint. A bad fault and the horse is necessarily light of bone. A horse can also be " tied in under the hock," giving an impression of a bad, slightly bent, hind leg. Also known as **Short of bone**.

Toad eye. Found only in the Exmoor pony. A distinct and wide mealy rim to both eyelids, and practically running round the eye, which is prominent, thus giving the effect of the eye of the toad.

Undershot Mouth. One which is deformed by having the lower jaw protruding beyond the upper with results similar to those caused by **Parrot Mouth** (*q.v.*).

Well-let-down hocks. A greatly prized item of conformation. The closer to the ground the hocks are (if unblemished), implying short cannon bones, the better.

Well-ribbed-up. A term signifying that the front or true ribs are flat, with the back or false ribs well " sprung " or hooped behind the saddle, thus providing heart and lung room.

Well-topped. An expression to denote a horse that is good in conformation above the legs.

INDEX

INDEX

253

INDEX

PRINTED FOR THE PUBLISHERS BY
WILLIAM CLOWES AND SONS LTD, LONDON AND BECCLES
781.360

5/12/6

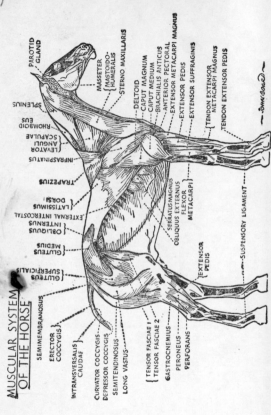

MUSCULAR SYSTEM OF THE HORSE

PAROTID GLAND

SPLENIUS

RHOMBOIDEUS

LEVATOR ANGULI SCAPULAE

INFRASPINATUS

TRAPEZIUS

LATISSIMUS DORSI

EXTERNAL INTERCOSTAL

OBLIQUUS INTERNUS

GLUTEUS MEDIUS

GLUTEUS SUPERFICIALIS

SEMIMEMBRANOSUS

ERECTOR COCCYGIS

INTRANSVERSALIS CAUDAE

CURVATOR COCCYGIS

DEPRESSOR COCCYGIS

SEMITENDINOSUS

LONG VASTUS

TENSOR FASCIAE 1
TENSOR FASCIAE 2

GASTROCNEMIUS

PERONEUS

PERFORANS

MASSETER

MASTOIDO-HUMERALIS

STERNO MAXILLARIS

DELTOID

CAPUT MAGNUM

CAPUT MEDIUM

BRACHIALIS ANTICUS

ANTERIOR PECTORAL

EXTENSOR METACARPI MAGNUS

EXTENSOR PEDIS

EXTENSOR SUFFRAGINIS

TENDON EXTENSOR METACARPI MAGNUS

TENDON EXTENSOR PEDIS

SERRATUS MAGNUS

OBLIQUUS EXTERNUS

FLEXOR METACARPI

EXTENSOR PEDIS

SUSPENSORY LIGAMENT